Pr(
Communi
Children with Down Syndrome

MW00974531

"Dr. Kumin's advice is simple, straight forward and down to earth, yet it is very sophisticated. She provides us with recommendations based upon up-to-date research and current leading theories without getting us into the academics of the professional field. Her book provides a great perspective on children with Down syndrome and their desire to communicate."

Michal Clark, Ph.D.
Past President National Down Syndrome Congress

⊞

"Communication issues challenge most individuals with Down syndrome. Dr. Kumin's informative, readable, and pragmatic work provides a rich resource for parents who strive to understand and expand their child's use of language. *Communication Skills in Children with Down Syndrome: A Guide for Parents* is a welcome and important addition to the Woodbine library of straight talk for parents about disabilities in children."

W. Carl Cooley, M.D.
parent and developmental pediatrician
Associate Director for Clinical Services
Dartmouth Center for Genetics and Child Development
Dartmouth Medical School

Topics in Down Syndrome

COMMUNICATION SKILLS in CHILDREN with DOWN SYNDROME

A Guide for Parents

Libby Kumin, Ph.D., CCC-SLP

WOODBINE HOUSE ⊞ **1994**

Published by: Woodbine House, 6510 Bells Mill Road, Bethesda, MD 20817; toll free 800/843–7323

Cover illustration & design: Lili Robins

Photo credits: pp. 10, 14, 30, 36, 46, 57, 87, 173, 187, 197, and 209— Michelle Sendler

Library of Congress Cataloging-in-Publication Data

Kumin, Libby.
    Communication skills in children with down syndrome : a guide for parents / by Libby Kumin.
       p.   cm.
    Includes bibliographical references and index.
    ISBN 0-933149-53-0 (paper) : $14.95
    1. Down's syndrome. 2. Mentally handicapped children—Education—Language arts. 3. Mentally handicapped—Means of communication. 4. Child rearing. I. Title.
RJ506.D68K86 1993
618.92'858842—dc20   93–29277
                                       CIP

Manufactured in the United States of America

10 9 8 7 6

Dedicated to

my parents,
Dr. Herbert and Berniece Kumin,
who have nurtured and supported me
and made me the center of their lives,

my husband, Martin, and my son, Jonathan,
who provide technical assistance and love
to help my vision become reality and who
make every day a truly memorable one.

TABLE OF CONTENTS

Acknowledgements .... **iii**

Chapter 1   Parents and Speech-Language Pathologists:
The Communication Team **1**

Chapter 2   Language, Speech, and Communication **7**

Chapter 3   Busy Baby—Busy Parents................................ **23**

Chapter 4   Before the First Word: Precursors
to Language **35**

Chapter 5   The One-Word Stage **55**

Chapter 6   The Two- and Three-Word Stages **79**

Chapter 7   Language Problems and Home Activities **97**

Chapter 8   Speech and Intelligibility Problems and
Home Activities **129**

Chapter 9   Understanding Speech and Language
Evaluation.. **169**

Chapter 10   Understanding Speech and Language
Treatment **193**

Chapter 11   Communication Needs in School and
the Community **217**

Index **233**

ACKNOWLEDGEMENTS

The people in our lives greatly influence who we become. My parents, Dr. Herbert and Berniece Kumin, have always made me the center of their lives. They have nurtured me and have served as examples of people who strive to make the world a more caring, responsive place for all people. My husband, Martin, and my son, Jonathan, have always encouraged me and have provided invaluable assistance as I learned to use modern technologies in my work.

My professional colleagues, the academic and clinical faculty of the department of Speech-Language Pathology, and the administrators, faculty, and staff at Loyola College, have provided a caring community in which I was able to grow as a professional. They have facilitated and supported my commitment to families and children with Down syndrome. Cheryl Mazaika Councill and Mina Silesky Goodman have been with me from the beginning of the clinical language intervention program at Loyola for infants, toddlers, children, and adults with Down syndrome. Our shared vision has developed into a vital, dynamic program because of our combined professional knowledge, but also because of our hard work and fellowship. John Sloan, Director of the Speech, Language and Hearing Clinics, has fostered the development of specialty clinics and has been a respected collegue and friend. The Green Family, Lynn, Jaison, Neal, Louis, and David, have been true friends throughout this project. Marilyn Miceli, Charles and Jason Kaufman were the moving force behind my early involvement with children with Down syndrome. Yvonne, Gene, and Timothy Proch, and Janis, Jay, and Melissa Silverman increased my dedication to children with Down syndrome and their families. To my professional colleagues with whom I serve on the Professional Advisory Committee of the National Down Syndrome Congress, I have considered it a privilege to serve with you, and my respect and admiration for your knowledge and commitment increases with each meeting. I would especially like to thank Dr. William Cohen, Nancy Murray, Margaret Lewis, Eleanor Hayden, and Lynn Green, who have provided insights as this manuscript became a book, and Marianne Burdett, who provided illustrations of a pacing board. Susan Stokes and Irv Shapell at Woodbine House have provided suggestions that have resulted in a more readable, user-friendly book.

There is a larger circle that has influenced my dedication and learning. Some of you I know by name; others I have spoken with only briefly. Some have come up after conferences or workshops to thank me. Others have sent photographs or notes or answered questionaires. You have made me feel that I have touched your lives and you certainly have touched mine.

1 | PARENTS AND SPEECH-LANGUAGE PATHOLOGISTS: THE COMMUNICATION TEAM

Communication is an essential part of living. We need to communicate with our parents, grandparents, siblings, friends, fellow students, teachers, and co-workers. We are always communicating, sometimes intentionally, sometimes not intentionally. We communicate when we say good morning. Our smile and bouncy walk communicate that we are happy. Our red eyes and sad face communicate that we have been crying. Our clothes communicate— the tuxedo and velvet dress say that we are bound for a formal event; the shirt and tie that we are ready for business. An infant communicates when he smiles at seeing a familiar face. A toddler communicates when he cries because he cannot reach the cookies. We communicate from the moment we are born, and continue to communicate throughout our lives. Whenever we interact with people, we communicate.

For children with Down syndrome, communicating is just as urgent and essential as it is for anyone else. Down syndrome, however, can cause a variety of physical and cognitive characteristics that make speech and language problems more likely. These characteristics include repeated middle ear infections; hearing loss; low muscle tone in and around the face and mouth; an oral cavity that is relatively small in relation to tongue size; over- or undersensitivities to touch in and around the mouth; and mental retardation.

Your child may face some, many, or all of these challenges. Children with Down syndrome have a wide range of speech and language abilities, just as other children do. There is no such thing as "Down syndrome speech." Each factor that can affect the speech and language skills of children with Down syndrome can also affect the communication skills of other children and adults. Some factors can be controlled or treated; others can be greatly helped by new techniques. This book discusses not only how each of these potential difficulties can affect communication skills, but also what can be done to help your child overcome them.

There are many people who can help children with Down syndrome master communication skills. Chief among these is the speech-language pathologist—the professional trained to understand the process and development of communication skills, as well as to assess and treat communication problems.

There are also many ways that you, the parent, can help your child improve his communication skills. As described above, communication *is* an integral part of life, so it is best learned as part of real life. As the people who spend the most time with their child doing real-life activities, parents are in the ideal position to work on communication skills. Parents are the primary teachers of infants, toddlers, and school-age children simply because they are the only ones who can carry over learning into daily life. Only the parent is there at breakfast, at bedtime, on trips to buy groceries or shoes.

If your child is young, the idea of being one of his primary communication teachers may seem intimidating. In reality, though, teaching communication skills to a child with Down syndrome is not that different from teaching any other child. It is true that you may need to take things more slowly, provide more practice, and put more conscious thought into teaching him. But you can also use many of the same techniques that worked with any older children you may have. For example, songs such as "The Wheels on the Bus" and games such as "Patty-Cake" can be just as effective in helping your child with Down syndrome learn communication skills as they can with any child. Likewise, involving your child in typical life experiences such as shopping for food, preparing for a holiday, or going to the beach can provide the basis for learning vocabulary and other language elements.

The major difference between working with your child on communication skills and working with a typically developing child is that you need not do it alone. You need information and guidance to maximize your child's communication potential. There are methods that facilitate the acquisition of speech and language in children with Down syndrome. The speech-language pathologist (SLP) can provide knowledge, information, insight, suggestions, and directions to help you. You, the parent, can also help the speech-language pathologist work more effectively with your child. You can provide him or her with information about your child's daily activities and feedback about how the therapy program is or isn't working. This will help the SLP design a therapy program that will best meet your child's unique needs.

Obviously, helping children with Down syndrome develop optimum communication skills should be a team effort between parents and the SLP. This book therefore has two purposes. First, this book is intended to give you some practical guidance in helping your child learn communication skills at home. It provides both background information about communication and Down syndrome and specific suggestions for home activities and home- and community-based language experiences, and also includes many suggestions for further reading. Second, it explains how to work effectively with your child's speech-language pathologist. It explains the process of communication, the professional terminology you may encounter, and the ways the SLP will assess and treat your child's communication difficulties.

In the end, I hope this book not only enables you to enhance your child's communication skills, but also opens the door to greater community participation for him. After all, communication abilities and community inclusion *are* related. I look at the many young children and their families in the speech-language therapy program at Loyola College and am amazed at how far we have come since I was a student in the 1960s. Today, these children and their families truly are experiencing life together and communicating with each other. This is clear from the excitement they show when they bring in photographs of their softball games, their experiences as flower girls in weddings, their roles in the school play, their participation in their church's winter concert, wanting to tell us about their experiences.

We have made the difference—parents, professionals, families, friends, and courageous young people who test their skills and try their best every day. Parents and professionals must continue to work together and advocate together because we share the same goal—to maximize the communication potential of children with Down syndrome.

Resources

American Speech-Language-Hearing Association
10801 Rockville Pike
Rockville, MD 20852-3279
1-800-638-8255
The ASHA is the national professional association for speech-language pathologists and audiologists. It has a toll-free information line that can provide information and resources, especially related to how to find services in your area.

National Down Syndrome Congress
1605 Chantilly Road
Atlanta, GA 30324
1-800-232-6372
The NDSC provides free information on all issues affecting children with Down syndrome. It also provides information and referral to local parent groups and comprehensive Down syndrome centers.

National Down Syndrome Society
666 Broadway
New York, NY 10012
1-800-221-4602
The NDSS provides information and publications relating to all areas of Down syndrome; publications are available on medical issues and the use of computers.

National Information Center for Children and Youth with Disabilities
(NICHCY)
P.O. Box 1492
Washington, D.C. 20013-1492
202-884-8200
800-695-0285
NICHCY provides free information and publications on all aspects of disabilities, including speech and language.

State Speech and Hearing Associations
Most states have associations for speech and language professionals. If you
need information about how and where to find appropriate services in
your state, you may contact your state professional association. State associations may provide resources, referrals, information, pamphlets, and
possibly speakers for your parents' group. The address and phone number
of your state speech and hearing association is usually available from directory assistance or by calling the American Speech-Language-Hearing
Association. For example, ask for the "Texas Speech-Language-Hearing Association."

2 | LANGUAGE, SPEECH, AND COMMUNICATION

Language, speech, and communication. You have heard the terms, and in general conversation, they are often used interchangeably. But, they really have very distinct meanings. The differences among the three are important to learn about in order to understand the abilities of children with Down syndrome and the ways children with Down syndrome can best learn to interact with others.

Communication is the process by which one person formulates and sends a message to another person, who receives and decodes the message. Man does not communicate by words alone. We can communicate through sign language, facial expressions, gestures such as pointing, and even Morse code and smoke signals. Even very young infants can communicate on a basic level by crying or making faces to let Mom or Dad know that they are hungry or uncomfortable.

When people communicate, they usually use a symbolic code. That is, they do not use the actual objects to relay a message; they use symbols that represent those objects. They do not, for instance, hold up a shopping bag to indicate that they are about to go to the mall. Any structured symbolic code that is used for communication purposes is known as *language*. Language is a structured system of symbols which catalogs the objects, relations, and events within a culture. Language is more specific than communication; it is a code which is understood by everyone in your language community.

Using language involves both receiving and understanding messages and formulating and sending messages. When we receive a language message and try to understand that message, we are *decoding* language; this is called *receptive language*. When we formulate messages and send them, we are *encoding* language; this is called *expressive language*. One of the ways of encoding and expressing language is through speech. Other ways of expressing language are through sign language, pointing to words or pictures on a communication board, or formulating written messages on a computer.

Speech is the process of producing sounds and combining them into words to communicate. It is the use of verbal output or verbal language. Speech makes it possible to be very specific. It is easier for you to know specifically what your child wants when she uses speech. When your child says, "I want apple juice," you know what she means easily; it sends a more specific and easily decodable message than pointing to the refrigerator would. But, speech is a more difficult system to learn and use. Speech involves the complex coordination of muscles. In addition to the ability to use oral language, speaking also involves the coordination of many brain systems to formulate and then produce the spoken message.

Of communication, language, and speech, speech is by far the most difficult for children with Down syndrome to use. This is because it *is* such a complex process, and children with Down syndrome often have difficulty with one or more of the physical and mental processes involved. (See below for an explanation of these difficulties.) Despite these speech difficulties, children with Down syndrome are often able to communicate their messages very well, especially in the early years. As infants and toddlers, they are interacting mainly with parents, loved ones, and a relatively small group of people who know them well, and understand the messages they are sending. These messages may take many forms. If your child points to the door or walks with you to get a cookie, she is communicating. If she cries or laughs or looks angry or hurt, she is communicating.

Children with Down syndrome clearly understand the concepts of language and communication very well and *want* to communicate from an early age. For this reason, it is essential that they be taught ways to communicate with, and have an effect on, people in their environment as early as possible. Communication skills should definitely not be postponed until your child can master the skills necessary for speaking. The next section reviews some of the difficulties your child may need to overcome in order to master various communication skills, while Chapters 3 & 4 explain how you can help your child communicate and master pre-language skills before she is ready to speak.

Speech and Language Characteristics of Children with Down Syndrome

There are many sensory, perceptual, physical, and cognitive problems that can affect the development of communication skills in children with Down syndrome. Your child probably won't have all of the problems described in this section, but she will have some of them. Identifying which areas are difficult for your child and which affect her speech and language development is very important. Identifying your child's particular challenges is the first step in doing something about them. Depending on your child's needs, specific techniques and information can be used to help her make maximum progress in communication development.

Sensory and Perceptual Skills

In order to develop speech and language skills, children need certain fundamental sensory and perceptual skills. Sensory skills include the abilities to see, hear, touch, taste, or smell objects and people in the environment. Perceptual skills refer to the ability to give meaning to this sensory input. Thus, the ability to hear your child's voice is a sensory skill; recognizing her voice and interpreting the sounds she makes as words are perceptual skills. Clearly, children need to be able to hear what is being said in their environment in order to learn speech and language. They must also be able to see and focus on objects in order to learn the labels of objects. And they must be able to receive and interpret touch sensations in

and around the mouth in order to learn how to make speech sounds. The sections below explore how sensory and perceptual characteristics of children with Down syndrome affect speech and language abilities.

Auditory Skills

The most efficient way to learn language is through hearing the language spoken in your environment. An estimated 65 to 80 percent of children with Down syndrome, however, have conductive hearing loss. This means that a problem, such as infection or fluid accumulation in the ear, is preventing sound from being transmitted effectively and consistently. The most common cause of conductive hearing loss in children with Down syndrome is recurrent otitis media, more commonly known as ear infections. Many infants, toddlers, and young children have multiple and successive ear infections, in part because they have small, narrow ear canals.

A conductive hearing loss not only affects the actual hearing, it also affects auditory awareness and listening skills. If your child doesn't consistently hear the sounds in her environment, she won't learn to pay attention to those sounds. She needs to hear the doorbell ring repeatedly to learn that this is a sound to pay attention to. Fluctuating hearing loss also affects phonological development or the development of speech sounds. If your child doesn't hear all of the sounds clearly, she may have difficulty learning the sounds. If she can't hear all of the sounds in a word, she may have difficulty learning to include all of the sounds in the word.

To minimize their effect on hearing, ear infections should be treated promptly. Antibiotics can often help to clear up ear congestion. In some cases, small tubes may need to be surgically implanted in the eardrum to allow fluid to drain away.

Some children with Down syndrome have sensorineural hearing loss. This is a more permanent type of hearing loss caused by damage to the inner ear, the auditory nerve, or both. It may affect the ability to hear at certain frequencies (pitches), and thus may affect the ability to hear certain sounds. Children with this type of hearing loss often need hearing aids to amplify sounds.

Because good hearing is so essential to speech and language development, your child should be seen regularly by an otolaryngologist (ear, nose, and throat specialist), a medical specialist who can treat hearing disorders, and an audiologist, who can evaluate hearing and provide therapy or assistive listening devices such as hearing aids.

Visual Skills

Children learn language by connecting a label with an object. To learn a word, your child must be able to look at you in order to learn how to say the word. She must also be able to look with you at the object or situation that the word is representing. For example, to learn the word "butterfly," your child needs to be able to look at you and to look with you at the butterfly perched on a flower. The ability to visually track, or follow a moving object, is also important in learning labels. Thus, to learn the word "dog," it helps if your child can look with you at the dog and follow the dog as he moves.

If your child cannot see clearly or has difficulty focusing on objects, she will naturally have more trouble learning to attach particular words to particular objects. Many children with Down syndrome have visual difficulties. At least 50 percent have strabismus, or muscle imbalance problems, that cause one or both eyes to turn outward or inward. Nearsightedness (blurred distant vision) and farsightedness (blurred near vision) are also a common problem.

These vision problems are all easily correctable and should not be allowed to interfere with your child's communication development. If you suspect a vision problem, you may want to consult a pediatric ophthalmologist—a medical doctor specializing in evaluating and treating vision problems of children. This doctor can test your child's vision even before she is able to talk and let you know how often you should come back for routine checkups.

Tactile Skills

In infancy, most children learn a lot about the world through the sense of touch, the tactile sense. For instance, when a baby is first handed a new object such as a block or a set of plastic keys, she explores it by putting it in her mouth.

Touch and sensation around the mouth is particularly related to speech development. Children with Down syndrome may have difficulty with sensory awareness. For example, if a child with Down syndrome chews a cracker or cookies, she will often not be aware if there is any food remaining between her lips, cheeks, and teeth. She will generally not use her tongue to clear the area automatically, but she can be taught to do this. She may also have difficulty with tactile feedback; that is, knowing where her tongue is and where it should be placed for a specific sound.

Children with Down syndrome sometimes have trouble processing sensations in their mouth which can eventually lead to speech difficulties. Some children have reduced sensation to touch in the mouth. Consequently, they may not enjoy exploring objects with the mouth and will get less practice moving the lips and tongue and may have more difficulty feeling where their tongue is touching when they try to make speech sounds. Other children with Down syndrome are oversensitive to touch (*tactilely defensive*) and may find any kind of touch around their face or mouth intolerable. If your child is tactilely defensive, you may notice that she doesn't like to be touched when you are giving her a bath, dressing her, washing her face, shampooing her hair, or cleaning her ears. She might not enjoy exploring objects with her mouth, and would get limited practice exercising the lips and tongue.

If your child is either over- or undersensitive to touch, consult an occupational therapist who is trained in sensory integration therapy. The occupational therapist can use activities and exercises to help your child learn to respond more normally to touch.

Sensory Integration

Much of language learning involves the ability to simultaneously process and organize input from more than one sense. For example, to imitate a word her mother says, a child must be able to hear each sound in the word and then figure out where to touch her lips, tongue, etc. to make those sounds. And to learn which words correspond to which objects in her environment, the child must be able to see what adults around her are talking about. This ability to organize input from various senses and apply them to everyday life is known as sensory integration.

A child's sensory integration ability often forms the basis for the way that we view the child and her behavior. For example, we generally judge whether the child is listening by whether she looks at us or follows our instructions when we talk to her. (That is, we judge her by whether she is able to hear what we say and then translate what she hears into the appropriate movements.) If we call her and she does not look up or respond, or if we ask her to come over and she does not move, we assume that she is willfully

not following our instructions. Not listening and not looking give a perhaps unfair impression of non-compliance.

Children with Down syndrome may need particular help in learning to pay attention, listen, look, and respond. One reason is that they may have trouble processing input from more than one sense at once—for example, if they are asked to look and listen at the same time. They may be overwhelmed by the many sensations around them—the pinch of their new shoes, the hum of the air conditioner, the smell of baking cookies—and be unable to focus on what is being said. Sensory integration problems of this nature not only make it difficult to learn communication skills, but many other skills as well.

An occupational therapist may be able to help your child overcome sensory integration problems. The American Occupational Therapy Association can help you locate a therapist trained in sensory integration techniques. See the Resources listing at the end of Chapter 2 for the address.

Physical Characteristics

Children with Down syndrome frequently have differences in the muscles or structure of the facial area that can result in speech difficulties. These differences include:

- low muscle tone (hypotonia)—muscles that are more relaxed and "floppy" than usual, and therefore more difficult to control. Muscles in your child's lips, tongue, and jaw might be affected.
- a mouth that is relatively small in relationship to tongue size.
- a tendency to breathe through the mouth due to enlarged adenoids or tonsils or to recurrent allergies or colds.

The problems above can all affect your child's *intelligibility* (how easily her speech is understood) in different ways. Your child may have trouble with:

- **articulation,** or the ability to move and control the lips, tongue, jaws, and palate to form sounds correctly and clearly;
- **fluency,** or the ability to speak smoothly and rhythmically;
- **sequencing,** or the ability to pronounce sounds in the proper order within words (for example, your child may say efelant for elephant or pasghetti for spaghetti);
- **resonance,** or the tone and quality of speech sounds your child produces (for instance, whether sounds are too nasal or "twangy" or not nasal enough).

Although the problems above can make speaking more difficult and frustrating for your child, they need not prevent her from communicating effectively. Chapter 4 explains how your child can learn to supplement speech with sign language until she is able to speak more intelligibly. Chapter 7 suggests ways you can work with your child on specific factors affecting her intelligibility.

Cognitive Characteristics

The mental retardation that accompanies your child's Down syndrome will affect her ability to learn in many areas. Mental retardation can have an especially big impact on communication skills, because so much of language learning depends on cognitive or thinking abilities such as reasoning, understanding concepts, and remembering.

Specific cognitive abilities that mental retardation can impair include:

- **generalization,** or the ability to apply information learned in one situation to a new situation. For example, even though your child might have learned that the plural of the words "dog," "ball," and "cookie" is formed by adding an "s" to the ends of the words, she might not be able to figure out that she can form the plural of a new word such as "dinosaur" in the same way.
- **auditory memory,** or the ability to remember words after they have been spoken long enough to process and respond to them. For instance, if you tell your child to hang up her coat, wash her hands, and come to supper, she may remember the first thing she is supposed to do, but not the second and third.
- **auditory processing,** or how quickly and efficiently your child takes in, interprets, and responds to spoken words. Children with Down syndrome generally need more time to process and understand what is said to them, and may therefore be slower to answer questions or respond to instructions even when they aren't experiencing auditory memory problems.
- **word retrieval,** or the ability to select the appropriate word in a given situation. This problem may affect the complexity, accuracy, or length of the phrases and sentences your child uses.

- **abstract thinking,** or the ability to understand relationships, concepts, principles, and other ideas that are intangible. Difficulty with abstract thinking may make it harder for your child to understand that words can identify the extremes of characteristics (hot/cold, short/long); that the same word can be used to label several objects that seem quite different (poodles, German shepherds, and chihuahuas are all dogs); that the meaning of a sentence depends on the order of words (Joe hit the ball vs. The ball hit Joe). In addition, your child may have trouble understanding and using words for time concepts like today and next year, and will tend to use concrete vocabulary, describing events and objects currently in her environment, rather than those she encountered at a different time or in a different setting.

These problems will have a significant impact on your child's communication skills, but she can continue to make considerable improvement all her life. As a parent, you can help by providing language experiences as the basis for learning language concepts, giving your child many opportunities to generalize words to new situations, and by giving your child plenty of practice in using new language skills. Later chapters explain how, specifically, to do these things.

Asynchrony of Language Skills

Children with Down syndrome do not achieve at the same level in all language areas. This results in what speech-language pathologists refer to as an *asynchrony* of language skills—some skills are more advanced than others. Most notably, children with Down syndrome are better at comprehending language (receptive language skills) than putting thoughts and ideas into words (expressive language skills). As explained below, however, there may also be other patterns of strengths and weaknesses.

Receptive-Expressive Gap

Children with Down syndrome can have auditory processing problems, as well as a variety of other difficulties, that interfere with language comprehension. Usually, however, they have far more difficulty expressing themselves, due to cognitive, motor, and other difficulties. For example, they often have difficulty sequencing words to express an idea or to ask for clarification when they do not understand something that has been said. This results in the so-called receptive-expressive gap. For example, an eight-year-old who has the receptive language skills of a typical seven-year-old may have only the expressive skills of a typical four- or five-year-old.

If your child is slower to formulate a response, you might assume that she does not comprehend what you said. You may need to wait longer for a response to find out whether she actually understood you or not. Do not assume that your child can't understand you just because she is slower to respond (or doesn't respond at all). She may need a cue, or a prompt, or more time to organize her response.

One consequence of your child's expressive language delay is that she will probably have shorter mean length of utterance (MLU) than other children. This means that, on average, her phrases and sentences will contain fewer words. At the age of four years, typically developing children have an MLU of 4.5 words, while children with Down syndrome at about the same age have an MLU of 1.5 words. By age six and a half, the average MLU for children with Down syndrome is 3.5. Although this may be a problem in school for academic learning, it does not have to be a problem in daily living. Most of the time, it is possible to get our meaning across with short sentences. In addition, environmental stimulation and language intervention do make a difference. Research has shown that parents who are trained to help their children learn language can improve their children's language skills, especially in the areas of mean length of utterance and structural complexity.

Syntax and Semantics

Two additional areas of relative weakness in children with Down syndrome are: 1) *syntax*—the grammar or structure of language (the order that different parts of speech take in a sentence and what function they serve); and 2) *semantics*—the meaning of words (including usage and understanding of vocabulary).

Research has found that children with Down syndrome have more difficulties with expressive and receptive syntax and vocabulary than do other children of the same mental age. That is, even though an intelligence test might show that your seven-year-old is generally performing at the level of a typical four- or five-year-old, her syntax and vocabulary skills would be lower than those of a four-year-old. Within these two areas, syntax is more impaired than vocabulary. Up to seventeen months, no difference is found between children with Down syndrome and typically developing children in syntax and vocabulary, but by twenty-six months, children with Down syndrome lag behind.

Although your child's vocabulary may be limited in the early years, studies have shown that children and adults with Down syndrome can continue to develop their vocabularies all their lives. The more experiences your child has, the more new words she will learn. There is no limit or ceiling to vocabulary acquisition, and the acquisition of new vocabulary words and concepts should be a focus from early intervention through adult life. It is true that your child will tend to use concrete words, especially nouns, because of her difficulties with abstract thinking. And she will likely use the same words over and over rather than using a variety of words, but if the words are appropriate to the situation, this may not be a problem in real life. Think of how frequently we say, "Hi, how are you?" or "See you later" without varying the structure. Much of communication is repetitive.

Pragmatics

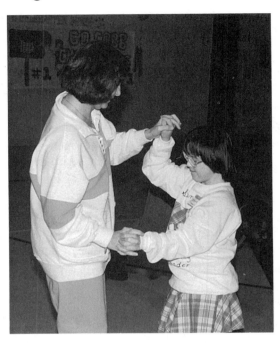

One area of language that is often a relative strength for children with Down syndrome is *pragmatics,* or the social use of language. Pragmatics encompasses such skills as using social greetings appropriately and understanding the unwritten rules of conversation (for example, everybody usually doesn't speak at once, but waits their turn). With practice and experience, children with Down syndrome usually do well in these areas. Children with Down syndrome also generally learn how to formulate appropriate messages for their listeners. For example, they learn to speak to their teacher using different vocabulary and syntax structure than they would use with their two-year-old cousin. In addition, most children with Down syndrome are skilled at the nonverbal aspects of pragmatics—for instance, making gestures and facial expressions to help people understand their messages. Other areas of pragmatics such as asking questions, requesting clarification, and staying on topic are more difficult for children with Down syndrome. With help from therapists and parents, however, they can usually make good progress in these areas. See Chapter 7 for suggestions for home activities. Working on social communication skills with your child is essential, as they contribute greatly to inclusion within the community.

Conclusion

Although the long list of communication problems that children with Down syndrome might have may seem daunting, much can be done to help overcome or alleviate the problems. As a parent, you can involve your child in activities and experiences that will help her overcome difficulties in many areas. And speech-language pathologists can use special techniques, materials, and exercises to give her the best shot at optimizing her communication skills. The next few chapters will focus on how to get started—how to begin the process of communication for infants and young children with Down syndrome. Later chapters will explain specific problem areas in speech and language, and suggest ways you can work on them at home.

3 | BUSY BABY— BUSY PARENTS

Your baby is home. There is much to do physically for him and for yourself. Besides recovering from birth, you need to adjust to the special needs that your child will have. Remember that your baby needs to be held and cuddled, fed and burped, changed and bathed, talked to and loved just like any other baby. Babies with Down syndrome are far more like other babies than different from other babies. There may, however, be additional medical or feeding concerns for children with Down syndrome. Seek information, find specialists who can help you give your baby a good start, and contact other parents who have walked the road before you. If you haven't already done so, enroll your child in an early intervention program where he will receive the specialized help he needs to maximize his learning. The special education department at the nearest elementary school or your local ARC can help you locate an early intervention program.

To learn and grow, every baby needs to have a wide variety of sensory experiences and to experience a stimulating environment. Interact with your baby from the very beginning. Talk to him, sing to him, rock him to music. We know that babies recognize familiar voices at a very early age and will respond. Put your face close to your baby when holding him; stare into his face while feeding. You want to begin to teach him the skills that are basic to communication development. This chapter focuses on the earliest skills that form the bases of language, and the feeding and pre-speech skills that help develop the skills needed for speech. The activities suggested are generally appropriate for babies with Down syndrome during the first six months of life. The time framework, however, may be different if your child experiences early surgery, or is tube fed rather than bottle or breast fed.

Visual Experiences

Infants learn a great deal by observing their environment, and especially by observing the people in their world. In the early months, babies are attracted by certain kinds of things in the environment. Research has shown that infants prefer bright colors, and can focus best on objects close to them. Research has also shown that the human face is one of the things that infants prefer to look at. Encourage your child to look at you, by holding him so that he can see you. Cradle him in your arms facing you. Hold him in the air with his face near yours. Smile, laugh, talk to him, and sing to him. Attract his attention to your face.

Once your baby is looking at your face, try to increase the time that he stares at your face. Make funny sounds or funny faces to stimulate him and keep his attention. Act as a mirror and imitate any movements that he makes. Use a full-length mirror, lie next to your baby and look at each other in the mirror. Make it fun for him to look at your face. And show delight in looking right at his face. The closeness helps him develop the skill of looking at you.

Be sure that the environment is visually stimulating. Hang colorful mobiles and pictures around the room. Encourage your child to look with you at objects around the room. Pick up a large toy animal or a giant beach ball, and hold it close to your child. Move it until you can see him looking at the animal and say, "Look at the ball. Isn't it big? It's fun to look at the ball!" Show delight in what you observe together. Have fun exploring the visual environment with your baby.

Sometimes babies with Down syndrome have more trouble focusing on faces or objects because of low muscle tone or difficulties in lifting the head. So, be sure to cradle and support your baby's head. Once you have him in a position where he can see your face clearly, he will want to look at your face and will delight in it in the same way as any other baby. Some babies will be more responsive, and will obviously enjoy looking at your face. Other babies may be less responsive. This is sometimes difficult for new parents. We all want feedback. There is nothing that is more reinforcing than a baby who smiles or laughs every time that your face appears. Some babies with Down syndrome take longer to show that response. But, the response will come. Your baby needs to see your face frequently and to be held close to your face and to see that you enjoy looking at him. Eventually, he will learn to look back, to recognize your face, and to think that it is a wonderful face that is special to him. This early visual training is very important. In order to learn to speak in later months, your child will need to look at you, and this is the beginning of that skill.

Auditory Experiences

To learn language skills, your child has to be able to listen— not only must he be physically able to "hear" but he must also be able to focus on sounds. Listening skills are developed through experience. You can help by providing many sounds for your baby to hear. Play music, sing, and talk to him. Try one activity at a time, so that your baby is not overwhelmed by too many competing sounds.

Play sound games with your baby. For instance, when he makes a screeching sound, imitate that sound. If your baby says "eeee," repeat the sound and then make it into a song. When your baby says "ah," repeat the sound and then repeat it again using a high-pitched voice or a very low voice. Your baby may have a short attention span and lose interest, so keep the practices short. He may also take longer to respond. But, it is likely that he will enjoy hearing you make "his" sounds.

Some other ways to train your child to hear sounds, listen, and increase his attention span include:

- Connect sounds with their sources. Make animal sounds for your baby's toy animals, and then ask, "What sound does the duck make?" Then say, "Quack, quack." Don't expect your child to join in the sound play for many months, but usually before twelve months of age, he will try to imitate some sounds.

- Use a variety of rattles, bells, and noisemakers to provide different types of sound stimulation and to attract your baby's attention. Encourage him to play with the sound toys, too. This gives him practice in hearing sounds and in exploring where those sounds come from.
- Call your child by name consistently. If he does not respond, attract his attention and then call his name again.

Remember that ear infections and fluctuating hearing loss may mean that sometimes it is more difficult for your child to hear your sounds, so he may sometimes seem not to be paying attention. On those occasions, make sure that he can see your face. Get close to him, and say the sounds more loudly so that he can see and hear you. And be sure to seek prompt medical attention for hearing problems, as your child needs to hear as well as possible to learn language.

Tactile Experiences

There are many tactile (touch) skills necessary for speaking. To speak, we not only have to be able to move our lips, we also need to be able to sense how our lips are moving: Are the lips tight together? Is the tongue applying pressure on the gum ridge? There are more sensory nerve fibers present in the mouth than in any other part of the human body. When your baby explores the world by putting objects in his mouth, he is activating this sensitive sensory system. As your child gains many experiences in infancy with touch, he also develops feedback loops. When he puts a toy in his mouth, or when he touches something soft and squishy or hard and solid, his body sends him information about those objects and about his mouth. These tactile experiences help build the tactile skills necessary to produce sounds.

Provide many tactile sensations for your infant. Rub and massage your baby. Use a towel to softly stroke or briskly rub the cheeks, face, and tongue to provide stimulation for your child. This helps him develop feedback loops for differing feelings of touch and also provides practice in localizing touch on different parts of the body. Face lotion can be applied to the cheeks and rubbed in, and games can be played touching the face and lips. For example, rub his lips, rub your lips. Bathtime is a natural time to do these activities, and once daily is sufficient. Let this be a special time of closeness that your baby looks forward to.

Encourage exploration with the mouth by providing sponge, rubber, or other soft, safe toys that can easily be put into the mouth and stimulate the lips, cheek, and tongue area. Provide a variety of textures in toys so that your child feels different tactile sensations. Soft toy animals with protruding parts such as dinosaurs or a giraffe are especially useful. Also encourage your child to explore his index finger, pinky, and thumb through sucking.

Rub your child's lips while he is drinking if he has trouble getting closure; massage under the chin. Encourage your child to imitate oral movements such as smacking the lips, clicking the tongue, and making funny sounds by holding your face close to his face while you make the sounds.

If your child is hypersensitive to touch and does not like to be touched, it is important to consult an occupational therapist. An OT can help your child learn to respond more normally to touch, and therefore make it easier for your child to learn to speak.

Communication Experiences

Several very important foundations to communication are laid during infancy. These include the concept of turn-taking and the knowledge that communication allows you to have control over your environment. As a parent, you play a central role in helping your child master these concepts.

All communication depends on turn-taking—on the fact that there is a speaker and a listener and that they can change roles. This is something that you can teach your baby very early through play and sound making. Although your child may need more practice to develop turn-taking skills, he will learn this skill and learn to use it correctly.

When your baby begins to make sounds, even crying or screeching sounds, imitate his sounds. Then wait, and allow him time to make more sounds. Sometimes children with Down syndrome are slower to take their turn, so be sure to give your child long enough to respond. You might want to position a mirror so your baby can see it, as babies often increase their sound play when looking in a mirror. Keep your face close to your baby's, and play back and forth with sounds. If he bangs his hand on the mattress, wait until he stops and then bang your hand on the mattress. Any motor movement or sound making activity can lend itself to turn-taking practice.

React to your baby's sound making as if it has meaning. Listen intently; when he stops making sounds, say "You don't say" or "tell me more" or "you want your bottle now, don't you?" Have a conversation with him. When your baby has taken a turn, you respond, then watch him and allow him time to take his turn. When he is able to hold a toy phone, have play phone conversations. This sound play is the beginning of conversational routines. Your baby will love having these conversations with you.

In "conversing" with your baby, use a high-pitched voice, use short simple sentences, talk more slowly, and use a lot of repetition. This is sometimes referred to as "motherese" or "baby talk." Motherese appears to help all infants—including those with Down syndrome—learn language. Once your child has reached the age of two to three years and has begun to use speech, some characteristics of motherese, such as using a high-pitched voice, will begin to feel unnatural or inappropriate. That's the time to fade out those characteristics. But, using shorter sentences and talking more slowly are characteristics of motherese that may be helpful even when your child is older.

For suggestions for teaching turn-taking to children above six months of age, see the next chapter.

To help your baby learn that soundmaking can influence his environment and get results, respond quickly to his cries and sounds. Help him learn that making sounds can bring him help. When he cries, pick him up, give him a bottle, or change his diaper, depending on what he wants. Talk about and respond to what your baby is interested in at that very moment. "Did you hear that airplane? It made a loud noise" or "You're wet, aren't you? We need to get a diaper very fast and make you dry."

Feeding

Feeding is an important activity in your baby's daily life. Not only does it provide him with the nourishment he needs to survive and grow, it also helps exercise the muscles needed for speech. This is because feeding relies on many of the same muscles that are used to produce speech. Through feeding, your baby gains practice in the movements of the lips, tongue, and other parts of the mouth

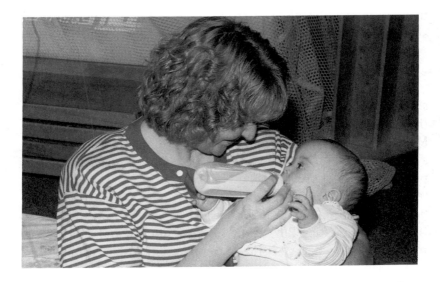

area that are needed for speaking. He also develops sensory awareness, perception, and discrimination within his mouth.

Sometimes children with Down syndrome have medical, sensory, or other problems that make it harder to feed, and, therefore,
to develop the movements needed for speech. For instance, low
muscle tone can make it harder to suck and swallow or to maintain
head and trunk control while sucking and swallowing. If your baby
has trouble sucking, a speech-language pathologist, occupational
therapist, or nurse may be able to suggest changes in the bottle nipple that will help. Some specialists have found that a preemie nipple makes sucking easier.

There are also some exercises you can do to help increase the
muscle tone of your baby's tongue. First, try tapping the tongue to
rhythmical music—bounce or pat the tongue with your finger, a
pacifier, or a teething biscuit. As the muscle tone increases, there
will be an increase in tongue movement. You can then gently
stroke your child's tongue to form a central groove or to move it
sideways or upward.

As your child progresses to semi-solid foods, it is important to give him foods with a variety of textures so he can continue to develop sensory awareness in his mouth and develop feedback loops for different types of textures. You might begin with foods such as baby cereal, applesauce, oatmeal, cottage cheese, and mashed potatoes. Gradually, you can introduce foods of different textures, including mashed fruit, soups, pureed meats, and yoghurt.

Once your child is ready for solid foods, you should be sure to offer him foods that encourage sideways movement of the tongue and biting. Foods such as Junior or chopped baby food, cooked vegetables, flaked tuna with mayonnaise, and spaghetti rings, as well as cookies and crackers such as zwieback, arrowroot, and graham crackers, may be introduced during this phase. Other foods that require your child to practice chewing and tongue movements are scrambled eggs, ground beef patties broken up, casseroles, small pieces of cut-up meat, raw fruits and vegetables, and small pieces of dried fruits.

Many children with Down syndrome have difficulty in shifting from bottle or breast feeding to cup feeding. Cup feeding involves different, more complex movements and greater muscle control. It may be easier for your child to begin cup drinking using thicker liquids such as thinned pudding or baby fruit thinned with water or juice. Thicker liquid is easier for infants to swallow. Your child may also have difficulty drinking when the cup is nearly empty. Typically, we bend our head back to drink the liquid from the bottom of the cup. This backward head movement causes some children with Down syndrome to choke. A cut-out cup will often make drinking easier. Cut a semi-circle out of one side of a plastic cup and have your child drink from the uncut side. When he tips the cup back to get the remaining liquid, the cut out provides a place for his nose and he doesn't need to tip his head back to drink. Cut-out cups can also be purchased from several companies listed in the Resources section at the end of this chapter.

If your child has a great deal of difficulty making the movements necessary for feeding, consult a speech-language pathologist or occupational therapist specializing in feeding therapy. Feeding therapy focuses on developing the muscle movements and the muscular coordination needed for safe and nutritious eating. If, on the other hand, your child is hypersensitive to touch in the mouth (tactilely defensive), you may need to find a therapist trained in sensory integration therapy. Otherwise, your child's hypersensitivity may cause him to gag or choke on foods, or to refuse to eat foods with certain textures. Finally, if your child needs to be tube-fed because he is not getting enough nourishment through oral feeding, it is important that the speech-language pathologist work with him on an oro-motor therapy program. The exercises and activities in an oro-motor therapy program will give your child practice sucking and swallowing, as well as making other important movements needed for later speech development.

Your Child's Learning Styles

The early months are the time to get to know your infant's learning styles. What are his preferences? Which sensory channels does he seem most interested in? What pleases him? Is he more alert in the morning or at night? When does he like to make sounds? Does he enjoy mirror play? Does he like to play in the bath? Does he like to listen to sounds? Does he like to look at an object or would he rather explore it by touch? What textures of food are most pleasing to him? Does he dislike certain textures of food? What activities are fun for you both?

Once you have determined your infant's preferences, you can teach him by working with his strengths and with what he enjoys. For example, if he likes music, you can use singing to help him relax during his "fussy" times. If he seems to enjoy looking around the room but does not look at your face, you can place your face closer to his, and give him more time to learn to focus on your face. If he seems to enjoy looking at his musical radio or his red stuffed dolphin toy, use those toys frequently. If variety attracts him, vary the toys. Enjoy each moment together as you begin the process of communicating together.

Resources

Books and Materials

Devine, M. *Growing Together*. Tucson, AZ: Communication Skill Builders. Early communication activities for you and your baby. Many of the activities involve father, mother, and siblings.

Getting a Good Start (1992) Available from DS Association of Greater Cincinnati; 1821 Summit Road Suite G-20; Cincinnati, OH 45237. Comprehensive discussion of early development of children with Down syndrome including information on how to locate and access services.

Hanson, M. (1987) *Teaching the Infant with Down Syndrome*. Austin, TX: Pro-Ed. This revised edition provides many ideas in all areas of development.

Morris, S. E. and Klein, M. D. (1987) *Pre-Feeding Skills*. Tucson, AZ: Communication Skill Builders. This is a very comprehensive and practical book, which not only discusses feeding issues, but also provides information on how to choose a pacifier, nipple, cup, etc. and how to adapt feeding when the child has difficulties.

Segal, M. (1985) *Your Child at Play: Birth to One Year*. NY: Newmarket Press.

Stray-Gundersen, K. (1986) *Babies with Down Syndrome*. Rockville, MD: Woodbine House.

Cut-out cups are available from:

Communication Skill Builders
3830 East Bellevue
P.O. Box 42050-E92
Tucson, AZ 85733
(Ask for the Flexi Cup)

Fred Sammons, Inc.
P.O. Box 32
Brookfield, IL 60513
800-323-7305

Organizations

The American Occupational Therapy Association
1383 Piccard Drive
P.O. Box 1725
Rockville, MD 20849-1725
301-948-9626

4 | BEFORE THE FIRST WORD: PRECURSORS TO LANGUAGE

You are undoubtedly anxious to hear your child's first word. But, many small steps need to occur before she even utters that first word. Each step represents a small triumph on the road to the first word. The skills on which language and speech are based and which precede language are known as *pre-language skills* or *linguistic precursors*. Each linguistic precursor is described in this chapter. Then, activities designed to help develop the precursor are presented.

Once you understand your goal as you practice the activity, you can vary the activity with your child. For example, if the goal is to have your child look at you and focus on your face, and your child seems to do that when you sing a specific song or make a funny expression, use those activities with your child. This practice should be done as part of your daily activities, not as a separate practice time because children with Down syndrome learn best when practice is a part of daily life. If your child appears to be frustrated or tired, stop the activity and do it some other time. Children with Down syndrome sometimes need shorter, more frequent practices because they often have shorter attention spans.

Prepare to be patient, but also to enjoy watching your child develop language. It is a fascinating learning process and you will see many areas of progress. Rejoice in the small gains! Let your child know how happy you are with her progress. Be generous with hugs and smiles. Within the first three years, most children with

Down syndrome can succeed in developing all of the language precursors described in this chapter with patience and practice.

Visual Skills

Reciprocal Gaze

Reciprocal gaze, conversational gaze, and communicative gaze are all different terms for what is commonly called eye contact. In American culture, eye contact is very important. People interpret looking at them as a sign that you are listening to them, and not looking at them as a sign that you are not listening or are uninterested.

Because of low muscle tone, infants with Down syndrome may find it more difficult to lift up their head. Visual difficulties may make it more difficult to focus on the face. So, you may have to provide more support for your child's head and neck, and compensate for visual difficulties as suggested by your pediatrician or ophthalmologist. But, reciprocal gaze is an important skill, and children with Down syndrome can practice and master it early in development, usually before one year of age.

Home Activities

- Hold your child so that you and she are facing each other. You might do this while sitting next to her crib, or holding her in your lap facing you.

- Initiate interactions with your child by physically moving closer to her, or by moving toward her face and then away from her face.

- When you are gazing into your child's eyes, make sounds or smiling or dramatic faces. Sing a short song or call your child's name. Do anything to get her attention. When you are finished, look away or move your child away.

- If your child doesn't look at you or fails to make eye contact, gently direct her face so that she is looking at you. Try to maintain her interest by singing, making funny faces, etc. so that she will look longer.

- When your child looks at you, assume that this is an initiation of reciprocal gaze. Begin smiling, or say "I see you."

- When your child is able to use reciprocal gaze, reinforce the learning through play. Games such as Peek-a-Boo, I See You are especially good. For older children, Simon Says, Hokey Pokey, and Head, Shoulders, Knees, and Toes promote reciprocal gaze.

Visual Tracking

Being able to visually follow the movement of an object (visual tracking) is an important skill in language learning. Your child will be better able to learn new vocabulary if she can look with you at a moving object such as a squirrel or an airplane as you name it for her. Children with Down syndrome often need more practice and more stimulation to learn this skill, but they are usually successful in learning it early in development.

Home Activities

- **Use a large attractive toy, such as a clown that has moving parts. Hold it right next to your face. When your baby looks at it, move it very slowly away from your face. Follow the movement with your own gaze. It helps to make noises as the toy moves to further attract your child's attention. You can use squeaking or noisemaking toys or you can make vocal sounds to accompany the movement.**

- **As you move a toy away from you and your baby, make your voice go up high. As you move the toy back towards you and your baby, make your voice go down low. Any interesting change in your voice will attract your baby's attention.**

- **Blow soap bubbles near your child, and pop them while you say "pop, pop" or point to them as they float away. The purpose of the activity is to watch the bubble and follow it as it floats in the air.**

Referential Gaze

Using referential gaze, your child looks at, and notices, an object. This type of gaze activity has two levels. In the beginning, your baby simply looks at an object. You may notice her gaze, and label the object for her. In the second phase, shared gaze, your baby watches you, follows your line of visual gaze, and looks at and pays attention to whatever you are looking at. This has also been called joint gaze, shared focus, joint attention, or visual regard.

Referential gaze is a very important visual skill for language. In order to learn the name of an object, your child needs to be able to look at the object when you are looking at it and remember what it looks like. When you label the object, your child needs to be able to look at the object in order to connect the label with the object.

Home Activities

- **Hold a bright toy near your face. When your child looks at you, squeak the toy. Move it a short dis-**

tance and keep looking at it. With exaggerated and dramatic voice say, "Ball, look at the ball!"

■ When you see a favorite person or a favorite toy, move your head obviously to look at the object, and say "Look, 'Daddy.'" You also can point to the person or object, and use a loud, dramatic voice to focus your child's attention on the object.

■ As part of your daily activities, name an object as soon as you see your child looking at it. Focus her attention on the object by using an animated voice or by searching for the object with your child, e.g., "Here's your bottle" or "Let's find the rubber ducky. Here it is."

Auditory Skills

Localization to Sound

Localization to sound refers to the ability to turn toward a sound source when you hear the sound. As your infant develops, she should not only turn, but also search for and fixate on the sound source. Listening to a person or several people in a conversation depends on the ability to localize sound and to listen to the source of that sound.

Home Activities

■ Use a variety of soundmakers: whistles, bells, cellophane crunched in your hand, hand claps. At first, make the sound in front of your child so that she can see what is producing the sound. Then produce the sound distinctly to one side of your child. If she does not turn, say "Listen," make the sound again, and say "What was that?" or "Look at that!" Then reveal the source of the sound. Make the sound so that she can see and hear it; then move the soundmaker out of sight and try again.

■ If your child has difficulty turning to the source of the sound, put her on your lap, facing away from the sound source. Produce the sound. Say "Did you hear that?" and turn your child toward the sound. Give her a reward such as a hug and a big smile for turning. Some children respond well if this activity is done with you and your child sitting in a swivel chair. When you hear the sound, swivel toward it and look directly at the source of the sound. You might say, "Here it is. Here's that bell we heard."

Attending to Sounds

When you know that your child is able to hear sounds, you can help her practice listening or paying attention to sounds. Your child needs to learn which sounds are important for her to listen to (people's voices, the telephone ringing) and which are not (the clock ticking, the refrigerator turning on and off). Otherwise, if there are too many competing sounds in the environment, your child might learn to tune out sounds, rather than listening to them.

Home Activities

- Play familiar sounds, such as the door bell, a dog barking, a favorite song that you have tape recorded. Watch your child's reaction. If your child is listening, she will generally stop moving or widen her eyes. When you watch your child, you will be able to determine what she does when she is listening. Comment on what your child hears. Say, for example, "You heard that music. It's pretty music, isn't it?"

- Talk to your child's grandmother on your phone, or talk to your baby from work. When your baby listens, say, "That's grandma on the phone. It's fun to listen to grandma, isn't it?"

- Make your voice the sound source. Call your child by name, or make a variety of sounds that will attract her attention. Move around the room. This activity can be used both to help her localize sounds and listen to sounds.

- Gradually, strive to lengthen the time that your child pays attention to sounds. Sing a longer song, lengthen the time of a conversation.

Motor Skills

Motor Imitation/Modeling

One of the most important ways young children learn is through imitation of those around them. Generally, children learn to imitate movements before they learn to imitate speech sounds. Although not directly re-

lated to language development, working on motor imitation is helpful as it teaches your child valuable imitation skills. Your child is usually ready for this type of practice when she can move her hand independently of other parts of her body. She may be swatting at her mobile, holding her own bottle, and exploring toys by using her hands to put them in her mouth. Some children will not be ready to imitate movements until they are able to sit up. Your physical or occupational therapist can help to determine when your child is ready for this type of practice. If your child does not seem ready or interested, wait a month and try these activities again.

Home Activities

- **Follow your child's lead. If she is playing with a toy and bangs it on the table, wait. Then, take the toy, and imitate your child by banging the toy on the table. Next, give the toy back to her. Demonstrate your pleasure in the activity by smiling and laughing.**

■ **The next time, you become the leader. You can roll a ball, push a truck, tap a xylophone, beat a drum, tap a block on the table, put a block in a box, etc. If your child does not imitate the movement, use hand-over-hand assistance, that is, hold your hand over your child's and demonstrate the movement by tapping the xylophone or pushing the truck.**

Motor Imitation Using the Body/Gestural Imitation

Once your child understands the concept of motor imitation, practice imitation using various parts of the body. This is a bit closer to imitation for speech because it involves motor imitation of parts of the body. Some of these movements, such as waving good-bye, will become meaningful movements later, but for now the goal is motor imitation. You may also add sounds to help stimulate your child and keep her interested, but remember that your child is not ready to imitate your sounds yet.

Home Activities

■ **Wave bye-bye.**

■ **Clap your hands.**

■ **Touch your nose.**

■ **Touch your toes.**

■ **Place your hands on your head.**

■ **Shake your head up and down.**

■ **Shake your head side to side.**

■ **Lick your lips.**

■ **Blow out your cheeks.**

■ **Open your mouth.**

■ **Close your lips tightly.**

■ **Pucker your lips.**

■ **Smack your lips**

Combining Motor Movements and Sounds

After your child is able to imitate movements involving the body, try getting her to add some sounds to the movements. These activities act as a transition to imitation of sounds for speech, because they provide practice in vocalization for your child as well as an opportunity to hear the sounds of speech in small sound bites. The discrete and precise movements needed for imitating speech sounds accurately are not yet developed at this stage, but will emerge later.

Home Activities

- **Blow your cheeks out and make a popping sound.**
- **Make circles on your tummy, rub, and say "mm-mm."**
- **Raise your hand in the air and say, "So-o-o big."**
- **Wave your hand and say "bye bye."**
- **Move a car and say "vroom."**
- **Move a toy dog along the table and say "woof-woof."**

Many hand-play songs are very appropriate for children at this stage. They enable your child to participate in speech or singing without really saying the words. By moving her hands, she is part of this activity. She can imitate the movements to the song, and later may begin to imitate some of the words. The Resources section includes some excellent books and tapes to help you learn hand-play songs such as:

- **The Bumble Bee Song**
- **No More Monkeys**
- **The Eensy Weensy Spider**
- **If You're Happy and You Know It, Clap Your Hands**
- **Where Is Thumbkin**
- **Here We Go Round the Mulberry Bush**
- **Hokey Pokey**
- **London Bridge**
- **Ring around the Rosey**

- **Ten Little Indians**
- **The Wheels on the Bus**

Pre-Speech Skills

Vocal Imitation

By the time your child is one to two years old, she will probably be ready to begin imitating sounds. Imitation of environmental and vocal sounds can give your child practice in making oral movements and in coordinating breathing and muscle movements needed later for speech.

If your child does not respond to speech imitation activities at first, go back to working on motor imitation with toys and sounds, as described above. Wait awhile and then try again with sound imitation. Your child will let you know when she is ready for sound imitation by responding and by being interested.

Home Activities

- **Smack your lips and make kissing sounds.**
- **Make crying sounds.**
- **Make nasal sounds, let air come through your nose like a foghorn**
- **Make sneezing sounds.**
- **Make coughing sounds.**
- **Make yawning sounds.**
- **Make happy sounds—cooing and "ahhh."**
- **Make environmental sounds: car motor sounds, beeping horn sounds, vacuum cleaner whooshing noises, etc.**
- **If your child has difficulty imitating or initiating sound making, try using a sound light. This is a light that is activated by sound—many electronics stores sell such lights or the materials to make them. The light will turn on whenever your child makes a sound and stay on only while he continues to vocalize. For added motivation, you can use voice-activated toys that will move as soon as your child**

makes a sound. Voice-activated toys are available from several companies listed in the Resources section or can be adapted from any battery-operated toy.

Imitation of Speech Sounds

Once your child has begun to get the knack of verbal imitation, you can move on to imitation of speech sounds. You should begin by practicing individual sounds used in speech and gradually progress to real words. Chapter 5 provides many more activities designed to help your child master single words.

Home Activities

■ **Make any of the speech sounds individually and repeat them—for example, /bababa/, /lalala/, /tatata/.* Try to vary the sounds that you use, but if your child is especially intrigued with the "p" sound or the "v" sound, stay with that sound. The easiest sounds to begin with are "p," "b," and "m," because your child can see how your lips move to make those sounds.**

■ **Take one vowel sound and vary the intonation pattern—that is, the sequence of pitches or the sing-song melody. For example, say "aaaah" with upward inflection and then with downward inflection, or sing "ahahahaha" with varying patterns. Take turns with you and your child being the initiator.**

■ **Say a familiar word such as "mama," "dada," or a sibling's name. If your child imitates the word, give a big reaction. Remember that the imitation will probably be approximate, so "grandma" may be "gaga." Always provide the correct model after your child's imitation, but don't correct her pronun-**

---

* Slashes are used to set off sounds or strings of sounds that go together. Speech-language pathologists often use slashes and brackets for this purpose.

ciation at this stage. Say, "Grandma, you said grandma; what a big girl!"

Early Pragmatic Skills

Turn-Taking Skills

As Chapter 2 explains, pragmatics is the ability to use language appropriately in social situations. Some pragmatic skills such as turn-taking—waiting for your turn—can be worked on in play, and will help your child master this important conversational skill even before she begins to speak.

Home Activities

- When your child can imitate a motor movement consistently, perform the movement, such as tapping a toy xylophone, then say "your turn" or "baby's turn." Give your child the tapping wand, and if necessary, use hand-over-hand assistance to help her tap the xylophone. When she is finished, take the wand back and say "Mommy's turn," and begin tapping on the xylophone.

In turn-taking, your child is adding on another skill to the skill that she has already developed in motor imitation. The goal of this activity is not to have her play the musical instrument accurately; it is to have her take turns with you. Keep your turn and her turn short, so that she learns about taking turns. Siblings who have learned to share can be great allies in this activity. You can demonstrate or model the activity using a brother or sister—Mommy's turn, Freddy's turn, Jenny's turn, Mommy's turn.

■ **Use motor games that your child enjoys. For example, roll a ball back and forth. As you roll the ball, say "My turn." As your child pushes the ball, say "Baby's turn" or use your child's name. Or you could send a toy car through a box tunnel and have your child send it back to you. Label as Baby's turn or Daddy's turn. There are endless variations on this game.**

■ **When your child can imitate a speech sound, wait until she finishes. Then say "My turn" or "Mommy's turn" and imitate her. When you finish, say "Baby's turn" or use your child's name, and let her take a turn.**

■ **Many infant game routines and songs foster turn-taking. These include Peek-a-Boo, Pat-a-Cake, This Little Piggy, etc.**

Social Communication Signals

Social gestures are body movements that are used to communicate. Usually they take the form of greetings such as waving hello or good-bye, shaking your head yes or no, or blowing kisses.

Home Activities

■ **Practice waving hello. Provide hand-over-hand assistance and help your child move her hand. Don't use imitation because your child will then probably wave backwards toward herself because that is what she is seeing. Wave hello consistently every time you see a new person or wave hello to objects in the environment. Say, "Say hello to grandma. Say hello to Uncle Fred," etc. Now, you are teaching**

> your child the meaning of hello as well as the gesture.

- **Do the same activity as above with the gesture for good-bye. Say "Say bye-bye to . . . ."**
- **Read a book with your child that highlights social gestures such as *Good Night Moon*.**
- **Use a puppet and say, "Wave hello to the puppet" when it appears, and "Wave bye-bye" when it is leaving.**
- **Practice waving with a brother or sister, going in and out of the room.**

Cognitive Skills

Object Permanence

When a child masters the concept of object permanence, she understands that an object still exists even though it cannot be seen. For example, she knows that her Raggedy Ann doll does not cease to exist simply because it is out of sight in the toy chest. This understanding is an important precursor for labeling through speech or through signing. Until your child learns about object permanence, she is not ready to give objects names. Before this stage, objects seem to appear and disappear from your child's world without rhyme or reason. When your child has mastered object permanence, she is ready to understand that a label not only is the name of an object, but it can also be used to symbolize the object when the object is not present.

Object permanence may be a difficult concept for children with Down syndrome to learn. This is because understanding the concept involves abstract reasoning, which is typically harder for children with mental retardation. Consequently, your child will probably need more practice to learn about object permanence. But unless she has a severe cognitive disability, she will probably be able to master this skill during the same age range that she learns the other skills in this chapter.

Home Activities

- Show your child a large toy. Hide the toy while your child is watching. Say "Where is the _____?" Then find the toy, and say, "Here is the _____." For beginning practice, musical toys are wonderful. Even when they are hidden, they can be heard, making them easier for your child to find.

- Move your child's hands in front of her face. Say "Where's baby?" Then move her hands away from her face and say "There's baby." This is an early variation of Peek-a-Boo.

- Play Peek-a-Boo. "Where's baby?" and "Where's Mommy? . . . Here she is." Children never tire of this.

- Hold a handkerchief so it only partially covers your face, or later on, hide under a blanket so it is obvious that you are there but can't be totally seen. Ask "Where's Daddy? Here he is."

- Hide a large object, such as a balloon, under a small blanket, so the shape and outline of the object can be seen, but the object itself can't be seen. Say, "Where is the balloon?" Children will usually delight in finding the object.

- Place the series of rings from a plastic stacking toy under a small blanket. Say "Where are the rings?" Let your child find the rings. When she locates the rings each time, say, "Here they are."

- Hide a small toy under a plastic bucket such as a sand pail. Look for the toy together by removing the bucket. Progress to having your child find the toy, and to increasing the number of buckets to two or three.

- Hide a small toy in your hand while your child is watching you. Say, "I'm putting the ball in my hand. I'm hiding the ball behind my back." Put your hand behind your back. Let your child see what you are doing and then let her find the toy.

- As you walk around the house, make a game out of finding familiar objects in their place. You might say, "Where's the apple juice? I found it. It's in the

refrigerator." After you pour the juice and put it back in the refrigerator, close the door. But, then re-open the door, and say, "Look, the apple juice is in the refrigerator." This helps with both object permanence and labeling.

Cause and Effect

This is the concept that an action has a result or consequence. Examples of cause and effect include flipping a switch to make a toy car move or opening a window to get fresh air. Understanding cause and effect relationships is vital to understanding communicative intent—that is, that when you make a sound or a gesture, your communication can have a result; communication can get you a desired result. Children demonstrate communicative intent when they point at the cookie jar to indicate that they want a cookie or say "Up" to indicate that they want to be picked up. Again, the concept of cause and effect can be more difficult for children with Down syndrome to understand because predicting the consequence of an action involves abstract reasoning. But with practice and repetition, you can help your child master this important concept.

Home Activities

- **Use toys that have a beginning and end sequence and a definite cause and effect, such as a Jack-in-the-Box. Turn the handle and the jack-in-the-box will pop out. Say, "Turn-turn-turn-turn . . . pop!"**

- **Use toy tops, especially visually interesting tops that have trains or cars circling inside. Say, "Go, go, go, go . . . stop." You control the movement so that the top stops when you say "stop" and goes when you say "go."**

- **Use busy box or pop-up toys; models are available with Sesame Street characters or Disney characters. When your child pushes a button or pulls a lever, a figure will pop up.**

- **Children often like to turn a light switch on and off, and see the results. This is a good example of cause and effect play. If you don't want your child playing**

with the room lights, make a play board with a switch and a small colored light or adapt a battery-operated toy so that when your child pushes a paddle, moves a joystick, or pushes a button, the toy will begin to move. An excellent source for information about adapting toys are the books by Linda Burkhart cited in the Resources section.

Means-End

Means-end is the concept that you can plan a course of action to solve a problem or reach a desired object. This cognitive ability, which develops over time, is one of the bases for the skill of planning a language message. The earliest means-end activities usually involve crawling to reach a toy that is out of reach. More advanced problem solving would be demonstrated when your child moves a chair to the counter in order to reach the cookie jar. There are three types of means-end planning:

1. displacement of barriers—for example, if a sand pail is in front of the toy radio, your child pushes the pail out of the way in order to reach the radio.
2. movement as the means—for example, your child crawls to a desired toy or walks to the VCR and starts the video he wants to watch.
3. use of tools—for example, your child uses a string to pull a toy or a stick to retrieve a ball that has rolled under the sofa.

Home Activities

- **Provide toys that promote means-end learning, such as pull toys that move along as you pull the string.**
- **Set up play situations that encourage your child to figure out how to get what she wants. For example, place the ball out of reach, and encourage your child to crawl toward it. "Come on over, come get the ball, come right over here," etc.**
- **Put a small barrier between your crawling infant and what she wants. Make the barrier lightweight and easy to move; a small inflatable beach ball, a**

balloon, or a transparent blow-up cylinder are good choices.

■ **Show your child how to use tools. Use a shovel and pail in the sandbox, and fill the pail with sand. Demonstrate or help your child with the action.**

Conclusion

The period before the first word is a very active period in language development. There are many home activities that can stimulate your child during this period. It is a wonderful period in which you can take the time to explore the world together with your child and enjoy the many learning opportunities around you.

Resources

Brown, M. (1947, 1977) *Good Night Moon*. New York: Harper & Row.

Brown, M. (1985) *Hand Rhymes*. New York: E.P. Dutton.

Brown, M. (1987) *Play Rhymes*. New York: E.P. Dutton.

Burkhart, L. (1980) *Homemade Battery Powered Toys and Educational Devices for Severely Handicapped Children*. Order from author at 8503 Rhode Island Avenue, College Park, MD 20740.

Burkhart, L. (1982) *More Homemade Battery Devices for Severely Handicapped Children with Suggested Activities*. College Park, MD.

Burkhart, L. (1988) *Using Computers and Speech Synthesizers to Facilitate Communicative Interaction with Young and/or Severely Handicapped Children*. College Park, MD.

Cass-Beggs, B. (1990) *Your Baby Needs Music: Music and Movement for Infants and Toddlers*. Ontario, Canada: Addison-Wesley Publishers.

Cromwell, L. (1983) *Finger Plays*. Livonia, MI: Partner Press.

Golden Sing-Along Series (1992). New York: Golden Books.

Manolson, A. (1992) *It Takes Two to Talk*. Idyllwild, CA: Imaginart Communication Products.

McConkey, R. & Jeffree, D. (1981) *Making Toys for Handicapped Children: A Guide for Parents and Teachers*. Englewood Cliffs: Prentice-Hall.

Raack, C. (1993) *EXCELL and EXCELL SONGS ON TAPE*. Tucson, AZ: Communication Skill Builders.

Schwartz, S. & Miller, J. (1988) *The Language of Toys: Teaching Communication Skills to Special-Needs Children*. Rockville, MD: Woodbine House.

Trube, B. (1993) *Tot Sock Hop*. Tucson, AZ: Communication Skill Builders.

Wee Sing Series (1982-1989). New York: Price Stern.

Equipment

Crestwood Company
331 South Third Street
Box 04513
Milwaukee, WI 53204
An excellent source for voice-activated and switch-activated toys to teach cause and effect.

Fred Sammons, Inc.
Box 32, Brookfield, IL 60513
1-800-323-7305
An excellent source for adaptive toys and equipment.

5 | THE ONE-WORD STAGE

When will my child begin to talk? This is a question that parents often ask. Generally, the words that you are waiting to hear will appear when your child reaches what is known as the one-word stage. The one-word stage begins when your child uses true speech—when he consistently uses sounds or word-like consonant-vowel combinations to represent objects and people or an alternative language system such as a sign to represent an object or person. In other words, this is the period when your child first says "momma" and "dada" and means *you*. Many children with Down syndrome say their first true words between ages two and three. Others may begin using speech between ages four and five. Still others may progress through a period in which they use both sign language and speech, or a communication board and speech, so it is very difficult to provide an average age for the first word.

The use of a word or symbol to represent the real object is the basis of language. When your child says "da" for daddy, "ma" for mommy, and "ba" for teddy bear, he is demonstrating that he has learned the code and understands the concept of true speech. That is, he understands that a word has meaning and that others will understand what he means when he uses that word. When we, as adults, use a word such as "table," the word has meaning because it is part of our language. There is no innate meaning in "table," no "tableness." "Table" is understood because we learned the code of our community as a child and everyone in the community uses the same code.

During the one-word period, most children's first words may not sound exactly like the word intended. For instance, an infant may say "ad," and use that sound combination consistently whenever he wants a drink. Eventually, his parents will figure out that he is using "ad" to mean apple juice. "Apple juice? You want apple juice?" they might say, assigning meaning to their child's early speech attempts.

Also during this stage, children often use one word or sound to mean more than one thing. For example, a child may sometimes say "ba" and mean "I want a bottle." Other times, he may say "ba" and mean "Take away this bottle" or "I dropped the bottle and I can't find it." It is up to the parents to deduce the meaning of the word based on context.

By interpreting their child's consistent sound patterns, parents teach their child that the world around him responds to his sound productions. Once a child grasps the concept that he is able to influence the world through his actions and especially through his sound-making, he will probably continue to try to get others' attention in this way. This is known as *communicative intent*—the knowledge that what you say will influence your environment and get results. Helping a child develop communicative intent is very important because it forms the basis for your child's motivation to communicate. Chapter 4 provides suggested activities to teach and reinforce communicative intent.

Children with Down syndrome are more likely than other children to have difficulty making speech sounds during this stage. As other chapters explain, this is because they often have low muscle tone in and around the face, hearing impairments, and other difficulties that make it harder to process and produce speech sounds. But even children with significant speech production problems can make important strides during the one-word stage. Their first "words" may be gestures rather than spoken words, but they can still improve their abilities in both receptive and expressive language. Often they learn to communicate through a system known as "Total Communication"—a method that combines gestures with speech sounds.

Total Communication

Although most young children with Down syndrome are delayed in speech development, they usually have relative strengths in motor development and visual perception. As a result, it is often easier for them to recognize and make gestures with their hands than it is for them to make speech sounds. Total Communication enables your child to progress in language, even though he is not yet ready to use speech, and overcomes his frustration at not  being able to be understood. Total Communication is the combined use of signs or gestures with speech to facilitate communication development. It has been demonstrated through research and clinical experience to facilitate the acquisition of speech. Total Communication is a method that capitalizes on the strengths of children with Down syndrome, and, for that reason, they should be taught using Total Communication as a transition language system to using speech. Not all speech-language pathologists are familiar with sign language systems or with their effectiveness with children with Down syndrome and may, therefore, not recommend Total Communication. However, research and clinical findings point so strongly toward the need for using Total Communication for children with Down syndrome that it would be wise to seek out a speech-language pathologist who can implement a Total Communication program for your child.

Parents are sometimes concerned that signing will prevent or delay the acquisition of speech, but the opposite is actually true. Without signing, children with Down syndrome—who can usually understand much more than they can express verbally—sometimes become very frustrated and resort to screaming or give up trying to be understood. By enabling your child to communicate, signing reinforces basic language concepts while empowering him to influence his world. An excellent videotape that presents the use of Total Communication from the parent's point of view is *The Use of Total Communication,* which is cited in the Resources section.

The sign language system that seems to be most often used for Total Communication is the Signed Exact English System (SEE). Another language system, called American Sign Language (ASL), has also been used with children with Down syndrome. Both systems use two hands for signing. ASL is a complete language with its own structure that is different from spoken English. For example, spoken English typically uses noun-verb combinations ("The boy runs") while ASL typically uses verb-noun combinations. In addition, ASL has no tense indicators. SEE, on the other hand, is spoken English in a visual mode. It merely translates spoken English into signs. SEE has a sign for most English words. Unlike spoken English, however, SEE does not have a language structure of its own. It only provides a way to communicate a message a child already understands, such as "more" and "help." Another system that may be used is Amerind, which is derived from American Indian signs. It has easily decodable signs which can be understood by 85 percent of the people who see them even if they don't know sign language.

The main considerations when choosing a system are your child's manual dexterity, readiness to use a sign system, and the prevalence of the sign system in your community. If he is in an early intervention program, you want him to be able to "talk" with the teachers and other children and get his needs met. You also want him to be able to be understood by siblings, daycare workers, grandparents, and significant others in his environment, and for them to be able to communicate with him. The purpose of using Total Communication is to provide a language system for your child so that he can communicate with others and learn that he can get his needs met through communication.

Whatever sign system is chosen, the first signs taught are usually "more" and "finished" or "no." These are powerful signs for your child to use. They help him communicate his needs, and enable him to control the continuation or termination of an event. Later, a sign vocabulary should be individually chosen to meet the needs of your child and your family. For example, if you live in a warm climate, "pool" or "swim" might be an early sign. Likewise, the sign for "sister" or "grandma" might be needed by a specific family, or a sign for "out" for a child who particularly loves the outdoors. The SLP will rely on you to let her know which signs you feel are important for your child to communicate. You might keep a list and discuss the needs with the SLP at the therapy sessions. You can rely on the SLP to teach you the signs and provide information on the use of Total Communication.

In general, the signs you choose for your child should:

- empower him and lead to improved communication;
- be functional so that they can be used often in his daily activities;
- be easy for your child to make.

Children with Down syndrome typically begin using Total Communication at about one year. When your child is able, he will generally begin verbally imitating your words while he is using the signs. Once your child is able to say the words, the signs will drop out of his repertoire. This usually occurs by age five.

Other suggestions for using Total Communication with your child include:

1. Remember that Total Communication includes both sign and speech models. Don't concentrate so hard on the sign that you forget to use the word.
2. Be sure that your child is looking at you when you present a sign or verbal model. Look at him when he is communicating.
3. Provide hand-over-hand assistance when teaching a sign. Place your hands on your child's and move his hands through the making of the sign.
4. Make sure that the signs you teach are meaningful and useful for your child in his environment and will be practiced as part of his activities every day.
5. Encourage your child to make sounds while signing, by repeating the word after your child signs it, but respond to the sign as you would to speech until your child is ready to speak.
6. Make sure that family members, day care providers, and significant others can understand and respond to the signs your child uses.

See the Resources section for books and materials on Total Communication.

Environmental Stimulation

Although your child may only know ten or twenty or thirty signs or words at this stage, that does not mean that these are the only words you should use with him. On the contrary, your child needs to be exposed to a rich variety of language all his life so that he can reach his potential in communication skills. Only by hearing many different words used many different ways by many different people can he learn how to communicate in the real world. This was proven in decades past when children with Down syndrome were all too often shut away in institutions, where they learned little, if any, useful language. All of the tremendous strides—the discoveries about the true capabilities of people with

Down syndrome—have occurred because parents now provide their children with stimulation, improved health care, and opportunities for inclusion and experiences.

Constantly stimulating your child's language can seem like a daunting prospect. But it is really not. Much of the language stimulation you provide your child can—and should—be worked into naturally occurring activities and routines. And you need not do all the stimulating on your own. Siblings, babysitters, grandparents, and friends will all be willing to help if you show them what to do. As an example of how learning can be incorporated into your daily life, here are some ways you might help your child learn the word "red":

Gather many red things from around the house—red towels, a red skirt, a red tie, baby's red stuffed fish, a red bell. Put them all in a "treasure" bag or a red laundry basket. Have your child pull them out one by one. Parent, sibling, babysitter say (and sign) "red" for each object as it is pulled out. You can make this an after-dinner game. Or, consider having a "red day." Wear a red shirt. Serve spaghetti and red fruit juice and strawberries and red apples. Go to the firehouse, where many objects including the firetruck are red. Read a book about red. Once your child has learned the word "red," put all of the objects back in place, go back to a variety of foods and regular daily activities. But every time a red item is encountered in the normal flow of daily routine label it as "red." When your child is able to say or sign the word, ask the question and provide immediate feedback: "What color is it?" (Wait for your child's response.) "Red. That's right. It's red." Provide additional practice with understanding the concept by declaring a "red" shopping trip where you buy only red items, or wrap a red gift basket in which all of the foods are red.

Teaching Words and Concepts

At the one-word stage, your emphasis should be on teaching vocabulary and concepts both receptively and expressively. Later on, you can work on pronunciation and grammar and pragmatics.

But for now, just focus on helping your child master important single words and their meanings. Below are some principles to keep in mind when working with your child on words and concepts.

Remember that language is more than spoken words. When you are teaching a word or concept, you need to focus on the meaning and on conveying that meaning to the child through play or through multisensory experiences with the word. Don't focus on the accuracy of the pronunciation. If you want your child to learn the concept of a car, ride in a car, talk about how a car looks and sounds, and play with toy cars. If it helps, use Total Communication and help teach the concept with a sign.

Provide many models. Children with Down syndrome need many repetitions and experiences to learn a word. When you are teaching the concept "in," for example, provide as many experiences as you can with the concept, and label the action each time. Put the block in the box and say "in." Put the apples in the bag and say "in." Put the bag in the shopping cart and say "in." Pour the orange juice in the glass and say "in." Put the envelope in the mailbox and say "in." Put the toy coin in the toy cash register and say "in." Clean up the toys and as you put each toy back in the toybox say "in."

Use real objects and real situations. When you are teaching a concept, use daily activities and real situations as much as possible to teach the concept. If you are teaching "drink", do it at snack time. If you are teaching body parts, do it at bath time. If you are teaching clothing names, teach while dressing your child or while shopping in a store. If you are talking about fruits and vegetables, teach while shopping in the produce section. Using real objects and experiences helps children with Down syndrome learn because they tend to have trouble with abstract thought. They may have difficulty understanding that a plastic apple or a picture in a book represents a real piece of fruit, but if they can hold, sniff, and taste a real apple they can more easily see the relationship between the word and the object.

Here are some suggestions and examples for teaching concepts as part of your daily routines:

DRESSING TIME:
This is a natural time for teaching about:
> Body Parts
> Clothing Terms
> Prepositions—in, on, off, open, close
> Verbs—button, zip, pull, sit, stand

MEAL AND SNACK TIMES:
> Food Terms
> Utensils—cup, plate, bowl, fork, spoon
> Verbs—eat, drink, chew, cut, wipe
> Adjectives—hot, cold, empty, full, all-gone, more

DRIVING OR WALKING:
> Vehicle terms—wheel, car, horn, stroller, truck, airplane
> Weather terms—cold, hot, wet, rain, snow, wind
> Outdoor objects—trees, sun, flowers, dog, cow, sheep, light, store, door
> Verbs—stop, go, open, close, push, pull
> Prepositions—in, out, up, down

PLAY TIME:
> Nouns—playground, ball, top, books, blocks, names of toys
> Verbs—kick, roll, push, pull, throw, drop, catch, stack
> Prepositions—in, under, on, through, up, down

SHOPPING TIME:
> Grocery Shopping—food terms, box, can, jar, big, little
> Clothing Shopping—hat, gloves, jacket, coat, shoes, socks, pants, skirt, blouse, shirt, sweater, belt
> Produce Shopping—Fruit and vegetable vocabulary
> Hardware/Houseware Shopping—trash can, lamp, paint, clock

BATH TIME:

> Nouns—body parts, water, duck, boat, bathtub, soap, towel
> Verbs—pour, splash, squirt
> Adjectives—wet, dry, hot, cold, big, little

BED TIME:

> Nouns—bed, blanket, pillow, light, bear, doll, door, window, moon, star
> Verbs—read, kiss, hug, close, sleep, cover
> Greetings—good-night

A comprehensive list of vocabulary terms and categories is included in the Appendix at the end of this chapter. This list can help you keep a record of your child's growing vocabulary from the one-word stage through the elementary school years. Simply check off the words as your child understands and/or uses them. You can also use the list to provide some suggestions for vocabulary words that fit under certain categories, such as items of clothing and weather concepts.

Teach, don't test. When you are teaching a concept, you want to provide models. You *don't* want to ask questions and demand answers. You *don't* want to go through stacks of picture cards representing the concept "in" and ask your child each time, "Where is the block?" You want to provide experiences, as described above. Language stimulation should not be "work." In fact, it is detrimental to set aside a half-hour for "practice" each day with a young child. After a while, the child "shuts down" and refuses to practice. Practice should be part of life and should use real objects and situations.

Reinforce the concepts with toy objects during play. Once your child knows a sign or word, reinforce the learning during play. If your child knows "up" and "down," use the Fisher-Price toy garage, and have the cars go up and down on the elevator, while you and your child say "up" and "down." If he is learning the names of foods, reinforce the learning through pretend shopping trips with toy food, a toy shopping cart, and a toy cash register.

Generalize the concepts. Children with Down syndrome frequently have difficulty generalizing—applying the skills they have learned to use in one situation to another similar situation. For example, your child may be able to identify the roses in your garden as "flowers," but have trouble understanding that the neighbor's daffodils are also flowers.

Provide many experiences with a word or concept once your child has learned the basic concept. Help your child learn, for example, that many different-looking animals can all be called "dog" and that many different things he eats can all be called "food." Label "car" so that your child learns that a red car, a blue car, a compact car, and a full-size car are all "cars." If you are teaching the body part "nose" and its function of "smell," say, "My nose can smell popcorn. What can your nose smell?" Keep the game up until you have named a dozen items that you and your child can smell. Comment on a smell when it occurs. For instance, in the bakery, say "My nose can smell bread." Use the game repeatedly over time, and your child will learn the concepts of "nose" and "smell" and be able to apply the concepts to many different situations. Do the same for many other concepts, including "bell, music, horn," and "dance, jump, hop, run."

Repeat what your child says. When your child attempts a word, repeat that word. Always provide a correct model when you repeat the word, but do not correct his attempts or make him repeat the word correctly at this stage. If your child says "ad" for apple juice, repeat it as "apple juice." Let your child know by your repetitions that you are listening to him and responding to his communication attempts. Repetition and responsiveness are very important.

Follow your child's lead. If your child shows interest in an object, person, or event, provide him with the word for that concept. If you are using Total Communication, ask the SLP at the next session to show you how to sign the concept, as well. Focus on your child's current interest and use that interest to teach your child new vocabulary or new sounds. For example, your child might show an interest in a toy ambulance at the toy store. Talk about the toy's color and size, what's in the ambulance, and that the ambulance has a siren that makes a loud noise. When you see an ambulance go by, point out the ambulance; or drive by the hospital to increase your chances of seeing an ambulance. Go to the library and take out a book about ambulances.

Follow up on whatever interests your child. When spring comes and the trees and flowers begin to sprout and grow, go for a walk with your child. If your child shows interest, go to the nursery and buy seeds or plants. Plant some flowers. Visit an arboretum. Read books about spring and plants. Use your child's interests to teach new concepts.

Practice active listening. Show your child through your repetitions, shared focus, and attention that you are listening to what he is trying to say. If you aren't sure what he is trying to say, guess. "You want a hamburger? You want a hug?" You will probably guess the meaning fairly quickly because you know your child's routines and needs best. But even if you guess wrong, you will still show your child that speech can get attention; he can influence his environment through speech. You will also show him that you value his communication and communication attempts.

Provide cues to help your child learn. Once your child understands a concept and is beginning to use the word or sign, provide cues or prompts when he forgets to use the word or sign, or appears to have difficulty getting started. These might include:

- *Physical cues*—Make a gesture or provide hand-over-hand assistance (actually hold your child's hand and put it through the motions) to help him point to a picture or make a sign.
- *Imitation*—Say the word for your child so that he can imitate your production.
- *Initial phonemic cue*—If your child is having trouble giving you the word or getting started, you can provide the initial sound, e.g. /b/ for ball, to help him. If you are using Total Communication, you might show your child the first hand configuration for the sign.
- *Fill-in sentence*—Provide a framework for the word by providing the beginning of the sentence or phrase. If you want your child to say "cookies," you might say, "You want milk and ____." This would be spoken with upward inflection, so that your child will fill in the space. If you want your child to say "shoes," say "socks and ___."

Use paralinguistic cues. These are the rhythm, stress, inflection and emotion in the voice, and singing-like production which can all help in teaching a concept. If you are teaching "big" and "little," use a deep, booming voice for "big" and a quiet, high-pitched voice for "little" while you are teaching the concept. Let your voice go up while saying "up" and down while saying "down." Commercials, advertising jingles, and "Sesame Street" all make powerful use of paralinguistic cues.

Conclusion

Children with Down syndrome can learn many different concepts and can continue to expand their vocabularies all through their lives. But it is during the one-word stage that your child first begins to lay the real groundwork for later language learning. As a parent, you can provide your child with experiences that will expand his vocabulary while teaching him about the many people, objects, and events in his community and his world. There are also many books that you can read with your child to stimulate language at the one-word level. Some good examples are listed at the end of this chapter. Remember, though: don't get so caught up in teaching your child that language learning becomes drudgery for him. If you can show your child that communicating is rewarding and enjoyable and that you value his communication, he will be far more interested in learning.

Resources

Crystal, D. (1986) *Listen to Your Child: A Parent's Guide to Children's Language.* New York: Penguin Books.

Dmitriev, V. (1982) *Time to Begin: Early Education for Children with Down Syndrome.* Greenbank, WA: Penn Cove Press.

Fowler, W. (1990) *Talking from Infancy: How to Nurture and Cultivate Early Language.* Cambridge, MA: Brookline Books (book & videotape).

Hanson, M. (1987) *Teaching the Infant with Down Syndrome.* 2nd Ed. Austin, TX: PRO-ED.

Holyhauser, P. (1986) *Language Learning Experiences.* Phoenix, AZ: ECL Publications.

Jenkins, K. (1982) *Kinder-krunchies.* Martinez, CA: Discovery Toys.

Manolson, A. (1992) *It Takes Two to Talk (2nd edition).* Idylwild, CA: Imaginart.

McCabe, A. (1987) *Language Games to Play with Your Child.* New York: Fawcett Publishing.

Schuller, J. & Seraydarian, F. (1988) *Step by Step.* Tucson, AZ: Communication Skill Builders.

Wiener, H. (1989) *Talk with Your Child: Using Conversation to Enhance Language Development.* New York: Penguin Books.

*Total Communication Resources**

Bornstein, H., Saulnier, K. & Hamilton, L. (1983) *The Comprehensive Signed English Dictionary.* Washington, D.C.: Gallaudet University Press.

Derr, J.S. (1983) Signing vs. Silence, *Exceptional Parent, 13 (6),* 49-52.

Dunn, M.L. (1982) *Pre-Sign Language Motor Skills.* Tucson, AZ: Communication Skill Builders.

Gibbs, E.D., Springer, A.S., Cooley, W.C. & Gray, S. (1993) *Early Use of Total Communication: Parents' Perspective on Using Sign Language with Young Children with Down Syndrome*(video). Baltimore, MD: Brookes Publishing.

Gustason, G., Pfetzing, D. & Zawoklow, E. (1980) *Signing Exact English.* Rossmoor, CA: Modern Signs Press.

---

* An excellent source of information is Gallaudet University's library, bookstore, and press. These departments provide a great deal of information. Call 202/651-5000.

Musselwhite, C.R. & Louis, K.W. (1982) *Communication Programming for the Severely Handicapped: Vocal and Non-Vocal Strategies*. San Diego, CA: College-Hill Press.

Skelly, M. & Schinsky, L. (1979). *Amer-Ind Gestural Code Based on Universal American Indian Hand Talk*. New York: Elsevier Publishing Company.

Children's Books for One-Word Stimulation

Single Word Objects

Carle, E. (1986) *My Very First Book of Food*. New York: Thomas Y. Crowell.

McGuire, L. (1991) *I Know My Animals*. New York: Little and Woods Press.

McGuire, L. (1991) *I Know My Foods*. New York: Little and Woods Press.

Ricketts, A. (1985) *Animals to Know*. Brimax, England: Brimax, Ltd.

Ricketts, A. (1985) *Look and Listen*. Brimax, England: Brimax, Ltd.

Ricklen, N. (1980) *Baby's Toys*. New York: Simon and Schuster.

Rockwell, A. (1985) *Planes*. New York: E. P. Dutton.

Seuss, G. (1970) *Mr. Brown Can Moo, Can You?* New York: Random House.

Simon, L. (1981) *My Toy Box*. New York: Simon and Schuster.

Simon, L. (1981) *Things I Like to Wear*. New York: Simon and Schuster.

Slier, D. (1988) *Farm Animals*. New York: Macmillan Publishing.

Wik, L. (1985) *Baby's First Words*. New York: Random House.

Colors

Burningham, J. (1985) *Colors*. New York: Crown Publishers.

Carle, E. (1986) *My Very First Book of Colors*. New York: Thomas Y. Crowell.

Fujikawa, G. (1978) *My Favorite Colors*. New York: Zokeisha Publications.

McGuire, L. (1991) *I Know My Colors*. New York: Little and Woods Press.

Hill, E. (1988) *Spot's Book of Colors*. New York: Putnam.

Pragoff, F. (1986) *What Color*. New York: Victor Gollancz.

Ricklen, N. (1990) *Baby's Colors*. New York: Simon and Schuster.

Seuss, G. (1963) *One Fish, Two Fish, Red Fish, Blue Fish*. New York: Random House.

Appendix

Selected Vocabulary and Concepts

Following is a list of basic concepts and vocabulary which are often tested in language inventories and are needed for school success and life in the community. Other terms will be needed in your specific family, school, or community. Add to the list, and use it as a jumping-off point to suggest other vocabulary words to work on with your child.

FAMILY NAMES

mom

dad

brother

sister

grandma

grandpa

aunt

uncle

cousin

VERBS/ACTION WORDS

drink

sleep

eat

kiss

hug

cry

come

go

see

go potty

put on

put away

hit

lie down

sit or sit down

stand

throw

catch

walk

run

pull

push

touch

wash

get

make

hide

tickle

swim

fly

tip-toe

hop

skip

wave

smile

laugh

yell

whisper

talk

blow

brush

pat

point

show

cut

paste

fold

write

list

number

CLOTHING

shoes

socks

hat

pants

shirt or T-shirt

sweatshirt

sneakers

dress

button

zipper

coat

snap

Velcro

skirt

jacket

boots

sandals

pajamas

nightgown

robe

underpants

undershirt

jeans

bib

apron

sleeve

collar

belt

tie

FOOD

milk
cookie
juice
apple
orange
banana
hot dog
carrots
potatoes
pears
grapes
salt
pepper
peanut butter
jelly
ice cream
cracker
cake
meat
soup
noodles
rice
spaghetti or pasta
ice
water
french fries
hamburger
steak
Coke
cola
soda or pop
peas
Jello or gelatin
pudding
beans
corn
eggs
bacon
sausage
pancakes
waffles
chocolate milk
sandwich
bread
rolls
potato chips
pretzels
tacos
butter or margarine
other food terms or specific brand and item names

BODY PARTS

eyes
hair
mouth
nose
ears
tummy
feet
arms
legs
hands
knees
fingers

toes

eyebrows

back

teeth

elbows

PLACES

home

synagogue

school

temple

day-care center

mosque

church

cathedral

grocery store or supermarket

doctor's office

hardware store

dentist's office

drugstore or pharmacy

fire station

bakery

post office

mall

hospital

toy store

restaurant

TRANSPORTATION

car or automobile

bicycle

truck

motorcycle or motorbike

van

vehicle

mini-van

ticket

airplane or jet

airport

train

train station

boat

garage

submarine

video store

ship

HOUSEHOLD ITEMS

spoon

plate

soup spoon

bottle

fork

key

napkin

toaster

placemat

toaster oven

tablecloth

can opener

cup

microwave

bowl

mixer

blender
food processer
pillow blankets

sheets
quilts or comforter

FURNITURE/HOUSEHOLD COMMUNICATION

chair
table
sofa or couch
desk
coffee table
VCR
videos
movies or films
dresser or bureau
night table
chest
closet
tape recorder
stereo or phonograph
CD player

pictures
lamp
bookcase or bookshelf
computer
television
telephone
radio
letter
refrigerator
oven
sink
dishwasher
washer and dryer
toilet
bathtub
shower

TOYS/PLAY EQUIPMENT/SPORTS

doll
ball
truck
car
teddy bear
book
bicycle or tricycle
baby carriage or baby buggy
airplane
slide
jungle gym
climbing bars
puzzle

swings
teeter-totter
skateboard
roller skates or roller blades
ice skates
tennis racket
sled or sleigh
skis
soccer
baseball
basketball
football

ROOMS/HOME

living room	basement
hall	deck
family room	porch
dining room	sunroom
kitchen	closet
bathroom	steps
bedroom	floor
attic	ceiling
carpet or rug	carport
drapes or curtains	game room or recreation room
garage	

SCHOOL

classroom	art room
open space/pod	speech room
gym	bathroom
cafeteria	cubby
playground	auditorium
music room	

SCHOOL/OFFICE EQUIPMENT

pen	desk
pencil	blackboard or chalkboard
marker	chalk
scissors	bulletin board
ruler	stapler
paper	paper clip
paste	diskettes or disc
glue	copy machine or Xerox
crayon	machine
paint	Fax
	computer

HEALTH/DAILY LIVING

soap

washcloth

towel

toothbrush

toothpaste

comb

hairbrush

shampoo

tissues

pain in ear/stomach

headache

cold

cough

water

hot

cold

ear hurts

clean

dirty

COLORS

red

white

black

blue

green

purple

yellow

brown

pink

orange

NUMBERS AND QUANTITIES

the numbers 1-10, 11-100

big

little

all

empty

full

more

less

many

few

most

least

a lot

long

short

wide

narrow

whole

half

almost

as many as

several

every

each

a pair

equal

PREPOSITIONS AND POSITIONAL AND COMPARATIVE CONCEPTS

top	on
bottom	off
in	same
out	different
over	alike
under	not alike
through	bigger
around	biggest
middle	smaller
in front	smallest
behind	away from
next to	right
inside	left
outside	forward
corner	backward
center	in order
row	beside
open	circle
closed	underline
center	below
side	above
before	put a square around
after	separated
between	together
up	skip
down	first
nearest	last
farthest	first/second/third
moving	high
still	low
next	beginning
toward	middle
away from	end

6 | THE TWO- AND THREE-WORD STAGES

The last chapter explored the wide variety of single words that your child will learn as part of a basic vocabulary. In the next stage, your child combines the words that she has already learned to make two-word and then three-word phrases. Children usually do not reach this stage until they have mastered at least fifty words. In my professional experience, children with Down syndrome usually reach this stage of learning sometime after four years of age. This is an exciting period when there are many opportunities for home activities for parent and child.

The Two-Word Stage

During the two-word stage, your child will be able to transmit a great deal of information. For example, she can make simple requests ("More juice"), describe her own and others' actions ("Daddy go"), and indicate possession ("Mommy coat"). Also during this stage, your child begins to learn the semantic (meaningful) and syntactic (structural) relationships between words. She learns that the order in which words are placed affects meaning. For example, the sentences, "The girl chases the dog" and "The dog chases the girl" may contain the same words, but they have two different meanings.Table 1 shows some of the many types of relationships between people and objects that can be expressed using two-word phrases. Note that—just as in the one-word stage—the same words may be used to mean more than one thing. For example, the words "no milk" may represent three different meanings:

REJECTION	I don't want any milk.
NONEXISTENCE	There's no milk here.

DENIAL   This isn't milk; it's juice.

TABLE 1
TWO-WORD PHRASE CATEGORIES

AGENT - ACTION	MOMMY PUSH; BABY PUSH (WHILE PUSHING TOY)
ACTION - OBJECT	DRINK JUICE; THROW BALL; GIMME BALL
AGENT-OBJECT	DADDY SHOE (AS HE PUTS SHOE ON)
POSSESSIVE	MOMMY CAR; SISTER DOLL
DESCRIPTIVE	BLUE BALL; BIG TRUCK
LOCATIVE (Place; Where?)	IN BOX; SLIDE DOWN
TEMPORAL	GO NOW; COOKIE LATER
QUANTITATIVE	TWO BALL; ONE CUP
CONJUNCTIVE (Goes together; and)	CUP PLATE; SHOE SOCK
EXISTENCE	THIS BEAR; THAT COOKIE
RECURRENCE	MORE MILK; MORE COOKIE
NONEXISTENCE (None Here)	NO BEAR; ALL GONE JUICE
REJECTION (Don't Want)	NO MILK; NO WANT; NO BANANA
DENIAL (This isn't)	NO JUICE; NO BABY; NO DADDY

Making the Transition to the Two-Word Stage

One of the best ways to help your child make the transition from the one-word to the two-word stage is to use *imitation with expansion*. Using this technique, you first repeat a word your child has said, then expand what she said by one word. For example, your child might say "car" while pushing a toy car on a play road. You would imitate "car" and then expand it by one word—for instance, "Car, car go." Or your child might say "ball" while looking around for the ball, and you could respond by pointing to the ball in the toy box and saying, "ball, see ball."

Imitation with expansion helps children learn how to combine words, and it provides the stimulation right at the level where they can learn. It is a technique that takes them from where they are into the next stage.

Three points are important to remember about imitation with expansion:

1. Repeat what your child says.
2. Validate that what she says is correct—demonstrate that you understand her and that she used a correct word.
3. Expand what your child says by one word.

You may present the imitation with expansion many times before your child begins to use two words; just keep at it. Repetition is essential; provide many opportunities to practice. This type of activity lends itself well to play and to activities of daily living. Once you get used to using repetition and imitation with expansion, it becomes an easy technique to incorporate into almost any activity, including eating, dressing, taking a walk, etc. You can also teach grandparents, siblings, babysitters, and others to use repetition and imitation with expansion with your child.

Imitation with expansion is just as helpful with children who use Total Communication as it is with children who use speech alone. To use the technique with Total Communication, you would imitate the single sign your child makes and then add another sign while accompanying the sign with verbalization. For example, if your child points to her glass and signs "more," you would sign and say "more, more milk."

Sometimes parents encounter difficulties in using imitation with expansion because their child may not initiate the first word. For example, your child may not talk as she plays, even though you know that she can speak or sign the words for the toys and for what she is doing with the toys. If your child does not initiate the first word, you can begin the conversation by talking about the activity.

Your child may then repeat one of your words, such as bear, and you can then expand what she said by one word. Remember, too, that your child may initiate conversations without using speech. For instance, she may gaze or point at an object. Whenever possible, follow your child's lead. You can respond to her initiations by labeling the object, and then expanding—for example, "ball, want ball." "Want" and "more" are always good words to introduce in two-word phrases because they teach your child to use communication to get *her* needs met.

One technique that you can use to help your child progress from the one-word to the two-word stage is the use of a *pacing board*. A pacing board provides a visual and tactile reminder of the number of words your child is able to use. The pacing board may consist of two colored dots on a piece of cardboard, two teddy bear

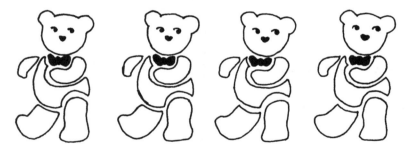

blocks put next to each other, a square of velvet and a square of sandpaper mounted on a board, two colorful dinosaur stickers mounted on a piece of cardboard—or anything else that your child likes. When you use imitation with expansion, point to the spots on the pacing board as you say each word. For example, in modeling the phrase "Car go," point to the first spot as you say "car" and to

the second spot as you say "go." Use hand-over-hand assistance to help your child get accustomed to using the pacing board for practice. Hold your hand on top of her hand and take her through the pointing motion. Using the pacing board provides multisensory cues—visual and tactile reminders for your child to use two separate words. Pacing boards are especially helpful for children with Down syndrome because they make use of the child's visual strengths to remind her to include two words.

At this point in her development, your child will probably not use appropriate word endings. For instance, your child will probably say "mommy shoe" or "daddy car" meaning possessive. When you provide the model, use the correct possessive forms, "mommy's shoe" and "daddy's car," but don't expect your child to use the correct endings. You might try to exaggerate the word ending by making it louder or more clearly articulated to draw your child's attention to the ending, for example, by saying "mommy'sss shoe."

Once your child is able to use two-word combinations, encourage her to do so consistently. Try to have day-care workers, grandparents, adult friends, family, and even siblings encourage your child to use two words. Give your child a big positive reaction whenever she uses two words: "You're so grown-up; you sound like a big girl now." This usually motivates children with Down syndrome to continue to use two words. If your child is tired, don't push her to produce the two words, but use imitation with expansion and provide the two-word model for her.

The section on "Learning and Play" offers suggestions on incorporating the learning of both two-word and three-word phrases into play. Also see the Resources section for books that discuss ways to combine language learning with play.

The Three-Word Stage

When your child is consistently using two-word phrases, you can begin to encourage her to use three-word phrases. This will enable her to express an even wider range of meanings, as Table 2 shows.

TABLE 2 **THREE-WORD PHRASES**	
AGENT - ACTION - OBJECT	DAD HIT BALL; BABY EAT COOKIE; I FIND BALL; SISTER KISS DOLL
AGENT - ACTION - LOCATIVE	MOM GO STORE; DAD COME HERE; BABY FALL DOWN; BABY GO BED
ACTION - OBJECT - LOCATIVE	DRINK JUICE KITCHEN; TAKE SHOE CAR; THROW BALL HERE
PHRASES WITH PREPOSITIONS	CAR IN BOX; HIDE UNDER TABLE; SOAP IN WATER; PUT IN BOX
PHRASES WITH MODIFIERS	WANT MORE CHEESE; SEE MY DOG; GET MY COAT; WANT RED BALL
CARRIER PHRASES	*I WANT* COOKIE; *I SEE* PLANE; *I LIKE* POOH BEAR; *I LOVE* MOMMY; *I WANT* COOKIE *PLEASE*; *I WANT MORE* JUICE

As before, you can use repetition with expansion to help your child progress from the two-word to the three-word stage.

For example, your child might say, "Car go." You listen and then repeat, "Car go." You have imitated, but have also validated the accuracy of her statement. Then you might say: "Car go fast" and make motor "vroom" noises, or you might say, "Big car go." As with the transition from the one- to two-word stage, a great deal of repetition and practice is needed, but the practice can be incorporated into play and daily life. In time, your child will use the words that she already knows from the one- and two-word phrases and begin to combine them into three-word phrases.

If your child is able to use three-word phrases, but doesn't seem to want to, try putting the three words to a musical tune. Say it very dramatically like an opera singer. Make it fun to sing the three words.

Two types of three-word phrases should be taught in different ways and therefore deserve special mention: carrier phrases and prepositional phrases.

Carrier Phrases. Carrier phrases consist of words such as "I want____ please" that often occur together in a particular order. They can be taught as a unit because your child will use them as a unit in daily conversation. When your child uses the phrase, he only needs to vary one or two key words. For instance: I want *candy* please, I want *play* please, I want *more cookie* please. Or: I like *Chris,* I like *Grandma*, I like *big drink.* Carrier phrases are very useful because they transmit a great deal of information. They are

also easier for your child to learn because they don't have to be formulated word by word each time she wants to use the phrase. She only needs to add the important word and her message will be understood.

There are many ways to practice carrier phrases as part of play. For example, you can use puppets, dolls, or stuffed animals to practice. "What do you like to eat for dinner? I like pizza. What do *you* like to eat? I like hot dogs." You could model the phrase using puppets, and try to get your child to imitate and then use the phrase. A toy grocery game or a toy fast food counter can be used for role playing to practice carrier phrases. For example, "What do you want to buy? I want soda. I want ice cream. I want peanut butter." Encourage your child to use the entire carrier phrase. If she uses only part of the phrase, provide the correct model, and try to have her repeat the model. You can set the phrase to a melody like a jingle, if your child enjoys music.

Prepositional Phrases. The other special type of phrase your child will learn during the three-word period is the prepositional phrase. Prepositional phrases begin with prepositions (relationship words such as about, around, above, across, in, under, through) and often provide the answer to a "where is" question. Examples of prepositional phrases are "in the box," "under the table," and "on the porch."

Your child will best learn specific prepositions if she can directly experience the direction and location they express through play. You might want to start off by using a big box and your child's entire body. Put your child *in* the box, *on* the box, and *under* the box. Then, use a smaller box and put a doll or stuffed animal in, on, or under the box while you label it "in box." Work up to asking your child to put the doll in or under the box. While you are playing, be sure to use different boxes (a shoe box, a gift box, a plastic box). You want to make sure that your child will be able to generalize what she is learning to different situations. If you always teach prepositions by putting the same block on, under, or in the same box, your child will tend to identify prepositions only with that situation.

Most playgrounds are ideally suited to teaching prepositional phrases. Your child can go *through* the monkey bars, *down* the slide, *under* the swing, and *up* the ladder. Again, be sure to provide many experiences, and to vary the equipment and situations to help your child generalize the concepts. When your child is able to use prepositions in speech, ask "Where do you want to go?" and then respond to her answer, whether it be "in the sandbox" or "on the see-saw." What if she answers your question with "sandbox" or "see-saw," even though you know she knows the prepositions?

Repeat the question, and then give the answer emphasizing the preposition by making it louder or more dramatic, e.g. "Where do you want to go? *On* the seesaw." Signs can be used to cue the preposition. An additional benefit is that the signs for prepositions, such as "through" or "between," look very much like the concepts they represent.

Language and Play

Play will be an important learning tool for your child during this stage—and indeed, all through childhood. As she begins to understand concepts, she will often play with toys as if they were the real objects. For example, she may pretend to drink from a toy cup (functional play), or pretend to feed a doll. Later, your child might build a bridge from blocks and have her toy car travel over the bridge (representational play). Play can be used as a window to observe your child's level of cognitive development. Excellent discussions of play are provided in *The Language of Toys* and *Adaptive Play for Special Needs Children*; both books are listed in the Resources section at the end of the chapter.

There are many ways you can use play activities to stimulate language development during the two- and three-word stages. Some tips to keep in mind are:

- Use your child's favorite toys.
- Follow your child's lead. Talk about and play with the toy that your child has chosen at that moment.
- Use imitation with expansion, validation, and repetition as you play with your child.

Here are some ways you might incorporate language learning into play activities at this stage:

- **Put a toy car in the elevator of a toy garage. Have the car go up and say "car up" or "car go up." As the car goes down the ramp, say "car down" or "car go down." Use a high-pitched voice as the car goes up and a low-pitched voice as the car goes down to further enhance learning.**

- **Use cooking activities—either pretend play or real "play." Make chocolate milk or spread cheese on celery. Use vocabulary at the two-word or three-word level; whichever is appropriate for your child at the time. Some examples are "in milk; stir milk" or "syrup in milk; stir with spoon."**

- **Use a toy shopping cart and pretend food. Put the food in the cart: "Soup in; cereal in; juice in." Then take them out at the toy checkout. This is a wonderful activity because it is so true to life.**

- **Use a large doll such as the My Buddy or Raggedy Ann doll. Dress the doll: "Socks on," "shirt on," "shoes on," etc. Children seem to relate well to a large doll and you can use real clothes and many of your child's own clothes to dress the doll.**

- **Use the *Motor Mat, Thomas the Tank Engine Village,* or some other town-like plastic mat. You can also make your own mat of felt or quilted fabric and customize it to represent your street or the landmarks of your town. Use the toy cars and travel around the**

village, talking about what you pass and what you see, the library, post office, supermarket, and park.

Play activities and reading activities are excellent ways to teach your child about questions and responses. In school, your child will particularly need to understand "Wh-" questions—the where, why, when, and who. As you play and as you read, ask your child "Wh-" questions. Remember to provide many examples of the answer. Model the answer—teach, don't test your child. Say, "Where are your shoes? On your feet. Where are your gloves? On your hands." When reading a book, ask "Where is the car? In the garage." "Where is the car now? On the bridge." "Where is Waldo? Behind the tree. . . ." The possibilities are vast, and play and reading are pleasurable activities for you and your child to share.

Language and Reading

Reading with your child is an excellent time to work on receptive language. Reading again takes advantage of the visual strengths of children with Down syndrome, and many children greatly enjoy reading. Sometimes, though, children with Down

syndrome have short attention spans, and may find reading too slow-paced. To help maintain your child's interest in reading, here are some suggestions:

- **Choose books that have large print, and colorful, interesting illustrations.**
- **Follow your child's lead and interests. Let your child choose books.**
- **Make visits to the library a regular part of your weekly routine.**
- **When your child has a favorite library book, purchase the book for your own home library.**
- **Choose books with thick pages that your child can turn herself.**
- **Make reading a special time. Try not to have interruptions. Make reading a loving time of closeness. Sit in a favorite chair, snuggle together, and read.**
- **Children love repetition. If your child asks you to read the same book again and again, read that favorite book.**
- **Read dramatically with expression, and show that you are enjoying reading with your child.**
- **If your child points to a picture or a word, follow her lead.**
- **Point to the name of the object in the book, point to the picture that represents the object.**

Many children with Down syndrome enjoy books about real activities because the stories are related to their real life experiences. You might read a book about autumn leaves, for example; then, follow up the reading activity with a real experience. Go collect leaves, do an art project with leaves, or make cookies shaped like leaves. Then re-read the book and talk about your autumn leaves. Or, write your own story, and help your child illustrate it, or take photographs to illustrate the story.

With a little creativity, you can probably think of ways to directly involve your child in reading other types of books. For example, you might choose books with an animal or a famous character

(Curious George, Big Bird) in it. Use a stuffed toy of that animal or character and act out parts of the book. Or you could select a book that focuses on sounds, such as *Mr. Brown Can Moo, Can You?* and together make the sounds that are described in the book.

After you finish reading a paragraph or a page, ask questions. Ask your child to show you who is jumping or where Grover is going. Have her point to the pictures in the book that answer the question. If you have a doll or stuffed animal that could represent a character from the book, you might ask your child to follow directions using the doll or show you the answer to the question using the doll.

If your child cannot answer your question, give her the answer. Remember, you are reading with her and teaching her, not testing her. If she cannot yet give the answer, try to have her imitate the answer. Emphasize the important word in your question— "WHERE was Grover hiding?" Once you have given the answer on several different occasions, try providing cues instead of giving the answer. You might give the initial sound of the answer, or give a phrase that will help your child say the answer ("j" or "He ate bread and ___" to stimulate the word "jam"), or use a signed cue to stimulate the word. Try to vary the way in which you ask the questions once your child is familiar with the content of the book. This helps in teaching and generalizing the concepts learned.

When your child is in the two- and three-word stages, she uses many modifiers. She not only says the one-word name of an object, but also talks about sizes, shapes, and colors. She uses adjectives and prepositions, and begins to talk about daily routines. And she learns to answer "Wh-" questions. The Resource section includes a list of some readily available children's books that may be used to help teach these concepts in expressive and receptive language.

Resources

Suggested Books

Prepositions

Berenstain, S. & Berenstain, J. (1971) *Bears in the Night*. New York: Random House.

Berne, P. (1974) *Where Is It?* New York: Random House.

Carlson, L. (1984) *Here Come the Littles*. New York: Scholastic, Inc.

Cartwright, S. (1983) *Find the Kitten*. Tulsa, OK: EDC Publishing.

Children's Television Workshop (1982) *In and Out, Up and Down*. New York: Random House.

Hill, E. (1988) *Where Is Spot?* New York: G.D. Putnam Sons.

Hoban, T. (1973) *Over, Under and Through*. New York: Macmillan Publishers.

Lund, D. (1970) *I Wonder What's Under*. New York: Parents' Magazine Press.

Seuss, G. (1963) *Hop on Pop*. New York: Random House.

Slier, D. (1988) *Where's the Baby?* New York: Macmillan Publishers.

Adjectives

Barton, B. (1986) *Airplanes: Big and Small*. New York: Thomas Y. Crowell.

Burningham, J. (1985) *Opposites*. New York: Crown Publishing.

Carle, E. (1979) *The Very Hungry Caterpillar*. Cleveland, OH: William Collins.

Freudberg, J. (1980) *The Count Counts a Party*. New York: Western Publishing.

Fujikawa, G. (1976) *Oh What a Busy Day*. New York: Filmways Company.

Rius, M. (1983) *The Five Senses: Touch*. New York: Barrons Educational Series.

Yorke, J. (1990) *My First Look at Touch*. New York: Random House.

Sizes

Dunlap, G. (1978) *Big or Little?* New York: Thomas Y. Crowell.

Hoban, T. (1985) *Look How Big*. New York: Greenwillow Books.

Hoff, J. (1982) *Large and Small Animals*. New York: Harper and Row Publishers.

Huntington, D. (1987) *What Size Is This?* New York: Macmillan Publishing.

Makin, C. (1983) *Sizes, Sizes, Sizes*. New York: Simon and Schuster.

Scott, D. (1972) *Do You Know Sizes?* New York: Simon and Schuster.

Yorke, J. (1990) *My First Look at Sizes*. New York: Random House.

Shapes

Burningham, J. (1985) *Shapes, Shapes, Shapes*. New York: Crown Publishers.

Eager, T. (1983) *Shapes and Sizes*. New York: Macmillan Publishing.

Harper, T. (1986) *Round, Square, Triangle*. New York: Macmillan Publishing.

Hersey, B. (1978) *Share with Us Shapes*. Brimax, England: Brimax Ltd.

Hoban, T. (1974) *Circles, Triangles, and Squares*. New York: Macmillan.

Oxenbury, H. (1987) *Shapes*. New York: Macmillan Publishing.

Pragoff, F. (1986) *What Shape Is This?* New York: Victor Gollancz.

Ricklen, N. (1990) *Baby's Shapes*. New York: Simon and Schuster.

Scott, D. (1972) *Do You Know Shapes?* New York: Simon and Schuster.

York, J. (1990). *My First Look at Shapes*. New York: Random House.

Daily Routines

Kunhardt, E. (1993) *Pat the Puppy*. Racine, WI: Western Publishing.

Dickson, A. (1983) *I Can Dress Myself*. New York: Western Publishing.

Dijs, C. (1988) *Little Helpers*. New York: Compass Productions.

Dunn, P. (1987) *Busy, Busy Toddlers*. New York: Macmillan Publishing.

Jonas, A. (1986) *Now We Can Go*. New York: Greenwillow Books.

Kunhardt, D. (1943) *Pat the Bunny*. Racine, WI: Western Publishing.

Kunhardt, E. (1984) *Pat the Cat*. Racine, WI: Western Publishing.

McGuire, L. (1991) *I Know How to Dress*. New York: Little and Woods Press.

Oxenbury, H. (1981) *Clap Hands*. New York: Simon and Schuster.

Oxenbury, H. (1981) *Playing*. New York: Simon and Schuster.

Rockwell, A. (1985) *In Our House*. New York: Publication Data.

Simon, L. (1981) *Things I Like to Eat*. New York: Simon and Schuster.

Slier, D. (1988) *Hello Baby*. New York: Macmillan Publishing.

Slier, D. (1988) *Little Babies*. New York: Macmillan Publishing.

Wh- Questions

Freschet, B. (1980) *Where's Henrietta's Hen*. New York: G. P. Putnam's Sons.

Gomi, T. (1977) *Where's the Fish*. New York: William Morrow & Co.

Handford, M. (1987) *Where's Waldo?* Boston: Little-Brown.

Handford, M. (1988) *Find Waldo Now*. Boston: Little-Brown.

Handford, M. (1989) *The Great Waldo Search*. Boston: Little-Brown.

Hutchins, P. (1990) *What Game Shall We Play?* New York: Greenwillow Books.

Hutchins, P. (1989) *Which Witch is Which?* New York: Greenwillow Books.

Kraus, R. (1970) *Which Mouse Are You?* New York: Macmillan Publishing.

Kraus, R. (1986) *Where Are You Going Little Mouse?* New York: Greenwillow Books.

Martin, B. (1983) *Brown Bear, Brown Bear, What Do You See?* New York: Holt, Rinehart & Winston.

Miller, M. (1988) *Whose Hat?* New York: Greenwillow Books.

Waber, B. (1967) *An Anteater Named Arthur*. Boston: Houghton Mifflin Company.

Watanabe, S. (1980) *What a Good Lunch!* New York: William Collins Publishers.

Weinburg, L. (1981) *The Forgetful Bears*. New York: Scholastic, Inc.

Weinburg, L. (1987) *The Forgetful Bears Meet Mr. Memory*. New York: Scholastic, Inc.

Weiss, N. (1989) *Where Does the Brown Bear Go?* New York: Greenwillow Books.

Zacharias, T. & Zacharias, W. (1990) *But Where Is the Green Parrot?* New York: Bantam, Doubleday, Dell Publishing Group.

Yabuchi, M. (1985) *Whose Footprints?* New York: Philomel Books.

Books about Play and Reading Activities

Manolson, A. (1992) *It Takes Two to Talk*. Idlywild, CA: Imaginart (800-828-1376).

Musselwhite, C. (1986) *Adaptive Play for Special Needs Children*. San Diego, CA: College-Hill Press.

Schwartz, S. and Miller, J. (1988) *The Language of Toys*. Rockville, MD: Woodbine House.

Trelease, J. (1982) *The Read-Aloud Handbook*. New York: Penguin Books.

Weitzman, E. (1992) *Learning Language and Loving It*. Idlywild, CA: Imaginart.

7 | LANGUAGE PROBLEMS AND HOME ACTIVITIES

The communication challenges for your child with Down syndrome will probably continue throughout his childhood. After conquering three-word phrases and short sentences, children with Down syndrome usually need continued help to improve upon the communication skills they have already acquired. The next two chapters discuss the communication problems and challenges of children with Down syndrome who already have basic speech and language skills. Understanding speech and language problems, playing with your child at home in ways designed to reinforce communication skills, and working with your child's speech and language therapist (discussed in Chapter 10) are the best ways to foster the growth of your child's communication skills.

As discussed in Chapter 2, communication ability is made up of many skills. This chapter covers language problems, such as incorrect grammar, and provides home and community activities to help improve language skills. Chapter 8 covers problems with speech intelligibility, and provides home and community activities to improve speech. Assessment of language skills, as well as professional treatment for language problems, is discussed in later chapters. Language needs specifically for school and the community are also addressed in a separate chapter.

Not all children with Down syndrome reach the three-word stage of language development at the same time. If your child is still working toward that goal, do not give up. Continue to work with him and to work with your speech-language pathologist. In time, most children with Down syndrome learn to speak in at least three-word phrases.

Language Development and Activities

Language is a very complex area because it includes many specific skills. As Chapter 2 explains, these include skills in the areas of 1) Semantics; 2) Morphology; 3) Syntax; 4) Phonology; 5) Pragmatics; 6) Auditory Skills; and 7) Advanced Language Skills. It takes a lot of time and effort for children to learn how to use language fluently. And, with children with Down syndrome, extra effort is required.

Children with Down syndrome may have trouble with all of the above areas of language development, or they may have trouble with only a few. Most, however, need help in almost all of these areas. The following sections describe the specific language areas and offer suggested activities for parents and older children in each area.

Semantics

Semantics is the study of meaning in language. It is what we call the vocabulary, or *lexicon,* of our language. Each language has its unique set of words for every object and concept. In American English, there are words for objects, and concepts like "ball," "help," and "good." Children learn by pairing the concept or object with the appropriate word. But with all children, including children with Down syndrome, we know it is not so simple. We know from studying the meanings that children assign to specific words that they often overgeneralize or undergeneralize when they are first learning the meaning of a word. For example, your child may overgeneralize by calling all animals *dogs,* or he may undergeneralize by calling only his red zippered jacket, *jacket.*

Semantics is sometimes referred to as the *content* of the language. Vocabulary is part of semantics, and vocabulary is best learned as it occurs in life experiences. This is especially true for children with Down syndrome. Vocabulary is an area in which children with Down syndrome do very well, and an area in which teaching by the family as well as practice and experience play a key role. The ability to understand and express vocabulary words as well as categorize them by concept (for example, fruits and vegetables, rooms and furniture) is important. Studies and experience show that children and adults with Down syndrome can continue to expand their vocabularies throughout life. Vocabulary gets your message across; with an extensive vocabulary and intelligible speech, you can get your message across even if you use short sentences or incorrect morphological endings.

There is an extensive vocabulary list at the end of chapter 5 which can serve as a source of vocabulary suggestions throughout the school years. You can also use it as a checklist to record when your child learns a word receptively and when he uses the word expressively. In addition, you can ask the SLP, preschool teacher, or classroom or reading teacher to send you information about what vocabulary is currently being used at school. For example, if your child is working on traffic signs, foods, seasons, careers, and community members, follow through at home. Visit stores, science museums, or the firehouse to provide real-life experiences that reinforce the vocabulary being learned at school.

Home Activities

- **Teach vocabulary concepts during a real-life activity. For example, when you are at the supermarket, name all of the foods that you see. Talk about what is in the produce section, what's a fruit and what's a vegetable, and name specific items. Have your child ask store employees where items are located.**
- **Reinforce concepts learned in real-life experiences by reading books. Take a trip to an aquarium as a family; then read a book about the aquarium and fish.**
- **Use a photograph album and "memory" photos to reinforce vocabulary concepts. During the summer, go to your neighborhood pool or park or to the**

> beach and label what you see; then use the photos
> to talk about the pool, park, or beach, and about
> the summer.

- Use your photographs from a family outing to create
  your own book. Mount the photos or draw your
  own pictures and create a custom-designed book for
  your child. Then, using the photos as guidelines,
  write a story together about your experiences on
  the outing.

- Categories are an important part of vocabulary. To
  teach and reinforce category concepts, take two
  carts when you go to the discount variety store.
  Bring 2 small signs; one saying "clothing" and the
  other labeled "appliances" (or "hardware" or any
  other category that you need to buy that day). As
  you shop, put all clothing into one cart and all
  hardware into the other.

- Teach children about categories by using objects
  first. Sort candy and toys into the cupboard and the
  toy box. Then use word games to teach both super-
  ordinate categories (generic categories like "fruit" or
  "animals") and subordinate categories (specific examples within categories like "orange," "apple,"
  and "banana"). After a trip to the zoo, ask, "How
  many animals can you think of?" or "A bear is an
  animal. What's a banana? Is it an animal? No, it's
  food."

Morphology

Morphology is the term used to describe how people use the individual elements of language—root words, prefixes or suffixes—to
form words. These individual elements are called morphemes. For
example, the root word "day" and its prefix "birth" and suffix "s" are
all morphemes. They can be combined into many possible combinations that convey variations of the root word's meaning, such as
"days," "birthday," and "birthdays." Morphemes are typically used
to express concepts such as plurals and present and past tense. For
example, the root word "walk" and the suffix "ed" are both mor-

phemes, and may be combined to form the past tense "walked." Words may contain one or more morphemes that are built on the root word. For example, the word, "phone" has one morpheme; the word "telephone" has two morphemes; and the word "telephones" has three morphemes.

Children learn the morphological rules of their language by listening to people around them. We know that children have learned a morphological rule by the structures they use in their own speech. When they use correct structures, such as "He walked," we know that they have learned how to convey past tense. But even when they use incorrect structures, such as "He runned," we can tell that they have learned the morphological rule for past tense, and are applying the rule, but just have not learned the exceptions to the rule. That comes with time and practice.

Children with Down syndrome sometimes have difficulty with morphology. In conversation, many word endings are said softly or unclearly, and children who have a hearing loss may have difficulty hearing them. Also, morphological concepts may be abstract, such as using "un" to mean negation or "—ed" to mean past tense, and consequently are more difficult to teach. Another complicating factor is that in speaking, children with Down syndrome often leave off final sounds, and many morphemes occur as the final sounds in words. For example, it is much easier for your child to say the word "bike" than it is to say the word "bikes." As a result, he may not get the amount of practice he needs to consistently know when to add the "s" to the end of some words.

If your child is working on morphemes in school or in speech-language therapy, ask which morphemes your child is working on, because you can practice with your child and can reinforce the specific morphemes being worked on in therapy. For example, if your child is working on the plural /s/ as in "chips," you can make chocolate chip cookies and count the chips, or you can go for a walk and find trees and flowers and birds. To practice past tense, you can describe actions on the playground such as, "I am jumping" or "I jumped."

Home Activities

- **Plurals can be worked on as soon as your child understands the concept of one and more than one. Work on plurals during daily activities such as folding laundry. "Here's a yellow sock. Here are two socks." Invent a game like "Go Fish." Try to put laundry items in pairs.**

- **When you go for a walk, point out multiples, such as flowers, birds, cars, trucks, and lights.**

- **Teach morphemes that involve time concepts through a real life activity. Cooking with recipes lends itself to this type of activity. For example I *will mix* the cake, I *am mixing* the cake, I *mixed* the cake. Be sure to emphasize the last morpheme of the word, the ending.**

Syntax

Syntax is the term used for grammar or the rules governing the form of the language. Syntax includes word order, sentence construction, and how to ask a question. As discussed in Chapter 2, syntax is a difficult area for children with Down syndrome because it is abstract, complex, and involves longer utterances. It is probably best to use home activities in the area of syntax as a supplement to classroom or therapy activities in order to focus on and reinforce specific skills suggested by the classroom teacher or SLP. Clinical experience shows that the areas of syntax that present difficulty for children with Down syndrome are: 1) the use of past tense, and agreement of pronoun and verb (for example, "He walks," "We walk."); 2) the use of personal pronouns ("he," "she," "himself," "herself," "his," "hers," "theirs"); and 3) active versus passive construction ("the dog chased the cat" vs. "the cat was chased by the dog").

Phonology

Phonology is the study of the sound system in language. For example, when a child with Down syndrome has problems with final sounds of words, this is considered a phonology problem. Chapter 8 discusses phonological skills in children with Down syndrome and provides many guidelines for home activities.

Pragmatics

Another important area of language development is pragmatics. It is important because pragmatics skills enable your child to use language to communicate with other people by conversing with them. Pragmatics is sometimes referred to as language *use*; it is the social and interactional use of language and can therefore be called real-life communication.

There are many different types of pragmatic skills. They include: 1) Kinesics; 2) Proxemics; 3) Intent; 4) Eye Contact; 5) Facial Expressions; 6) Conversational Skills; 7) Stylistic Variations; 8) Presuppositions; 9) Turn-Taking; 10) Topicalization; 11) Requests; and 12) Clarification and Repairs. The following sections explain each of these areas of pragmatics.

Kinesics. Kinesics is the use of gestures in communication. Pointing to a cookie in the bakery or circling your fingers for the "OK" sign are examples of kinesics. Gestures can support and reinforce communication. For example, people shake their fingers to indicate that they are angry and shrug their shoulders to show that there is nothing they can do. Gestures can also replace communication; for example, when your child waves across the playground or when your mouth is full and someone asks if you want more pasta and you shake your head "yes." Gestures are learned primarily through imitation. Different cultures have different gestures, and your child learns his set of gestures from the people around him. In my work with children with Down syndrome, I have observed that they do not have difficulty with gestures, and usually use them appropriately when they have lots of practice at home and in the community.

Home Activities

- Play "Show Me." Ask your child a series of questions and allow him to answer with gestures only. For example, "Where is your ATV truck?" "Do you want to go to the store now?" Then change places; have your child ask you questions that you answer only with gestures.

- "Yes, No, I Don't Know Game." Ask a series of questions that can be answered only by yes or no. Your child has to answer by moving his head only. If he doesn't know the answer, he has to shrug his shoulders and make the facial expressions for "I don't know." Involve siblings and friends in this game, and make some of the questions funny, to make this practice a game rather than work.

- Pointing is a very specific gesture that language experts call *deixis*. Play the game "Where is It?" Using household objects, ask "Where is the telephone?" Your child needs to answer by pointing. For older children, use cards depicting various rooms, and have your child point to the room. For example, "Where is the blue quilt? Where is the dishwasher?"

- Deixis can be practiced using games. You can also make a gameboard. In the center of the gameboard, have small photos of many objects in your house. Your child rolls dice, moves his gamepiece the correct number of spaces, and lands on a room name or picture. He then has to *point* to the object in the center of the board that goes in that room. This is also good practice for associations and categories for receptive language. Vary the gameboard and the pictures to include outside activities your child enjoys such as baseball, soccer, or camping.

Proxemics. Proxemics is how a person uses space and distance in interpersonal situations. It includes personal posture, how close we stand to another person, and touch and physical contact. Proxemics vary greatly from culture to culture and even from one geographic region to another. In some cultures, men kiss or hug and women hold hands or walk arm in arm; in others this would be considered inappropriate. There is no right and wrong in proxemics; there is only what is appropriate behavior in a situation and what is inappropriate. Parents usually work with children to ensure culturally appropriate behavior.

The most common problem children with Down syndrome have with proxemics is maintaining appropriate physical distance from strangers or acquaintances. Children with Down syndrome tend to get physically close, hug, and show affection when they may not know the person well. In my heart, I view this as a strength, as a reflection of the warmth and love that children with Down syndrome feel. But, as children become adolescents, inappropriate hugging or closeness can get them into trouble. It is important to preserve closeness, but just help ensure it occurs at appropriate times with appropriate people.

Parents of children with Down syndrome need to start early to work on proxemics and always keep in mind what is appropriate adult behavior within their culture. For example, strangers may find it cute if a four-year-old with Down syndrome comes up to them and gives them a hug, but the same people will find it intimidating if a male teenager with Down syndrome comes up to give them a hug. It helps if you help your child understand who is a stranger, who is a friend, and who is a close friend, and what is appropriate behavior. Practice at home and practice in the community to help your child learn what is appropriate.

Home Activities

■ **Role playing and acting out real-life situations are terrific ways to teach and practice proxemics at home. Set up a scenario such as going to a fast food restaurant. Use props such as fast food restaurant hats and menus to set the stage. Role play what you would do in the situation. For example, act out waiting in line and talking to employees and customers.**

Talk about what is appropriate physical distance and behavior.

■ **Another scenario might be going to the video store to rent a movie. Act out waiting in line, ordering the video, not pushing in front, and responding if someone cuts in front of you in line.**

Intent. Intent is the term used to describe the purpose of the conversation. If your child's intent and the message received by the listener are the same, the intent has been successfully communicated. For example, your child says, "I like to watch *Star Wars,* but no more." You might say, "Would you like to go rent another video?" If your child's intent was to go rent a different video, he has communicated his intent to you successfully. Intent doesn't even have to involve speech; your child's communicative purpose may be shown through his getting his coat to show you that he wants to go out. You want to encourage communicative intent; using communication to get your needs met. Here are activities to help:

• With an older child, comment on his verbal and non-verbal intent. For example, "I can see that you're watching for the ice cream truck. Do you want to ask me something?" If you get no response ask, "Do you want an ice cream pop?" Or, "You really like to listen to that song on the radio. Do you want to ask me anything?" If you get no response, ask, "Would you like to buy the tape?"

• Intent may be practiced as part of "scripts" or "routines." Talk with your child about the "purpose" of a phone call or errand. "We are calling directory assistance to get Freddy's phone number," or "We need to return these pants because they are too small. We will tell the salesperson that they are small, and that we need to buy a bigger size." Use frequent reminders if your child forgets what he was planning to say. During practice, it is even fine to use cue cards; they can have words, photographs, or pictured reminders on them.

Eye Contact. Eye contact plays a critical role in social communication. In some cultures, direct eye contact is considered very important. People will say, "Can't you look at me when I talk to you?" or make comments like "He looked me right in the eye; I could tell he was an honest person." When you are listening and when you are talking, it is considered appropriate to look at the other person. If you are in a group, you are expected to look at the person who is speaking. In other cultures, however, it is considered a sign of respect to look away and is considered aggressive to look directly at another person. So, what is considered appropriate eye contact varies between cultures.

To be accepted, it is important to use the eye contact patterns considered appropriate in your culture. Until children with Down syndrome learn that direct eye contact is expected in school, they may be incorrectly labeled as inattentive or unmotivated. Children with Down syndrome often look down, or do not look people in the eye. This is a skill that can be practiced at home.

Home Activities

- **Play a "Look Me in the Eye" game. Every time your child looks you in the eye, make a secret signal such as a wink.**

- **Place a sticker on your forehead. Your child has to look you in the eye and name the sticker.**

- **Create a special pair of handmade or purchased eyeglasses that you call the "Look at My Eyes" glasses. These may be funny and wildly decorated. When wearing the glasses, your child must look everyone in the eye. Use additional pairs for siblings and friends who can also participate in this game. Have your child wear the glasses for five minutes each day, and increase the time gradually.**

Facial Expressions. According to communications researchers, about 38 percent of the meaning of your message is communicated through facial expressions. So, they are a very important part of communication. Research has also shown that there are universal facial expressions such as happiness, grief, and anger. But, what triggers these emotions will vary from culture to culture. What is important is that the facial expressions match the message being sent. For example, if I say, "I love camp" and I am smiling and look happy, it reinforces my verbal message. But, what happens if I look sad and if my voice sounds sad or angry even though I am saying "I love camp." Research has shown that the listener will believe the non-verbal message if the verbal and nonverbal messages being sent don't agree. So, I would believe that you really don't like camp if you look and sound unhappy.

Children with Down syndrome are often very adept at reading people's emotions. They might know immediately that you're feeling sad. However, children with Down syndrome sometimes have difficulty reading facial expressions. For example, when your child is joking around with his brother and you intervene because it is time to get ready to go to sleep, your child with Down syndrome may persist in joking around and miss your facial expressions that show you are becoming increasingly annoyed. You can help your child by providing a verbal cue, such as "I'm getting annoyed. It's not time to joke anymore; it's time to go to sleep. Can you see my face? I'm getting angry." Practice can help your child learn to tune in to facial expressions and interpret them. It is very important for your child with Down syndrome to be able to understand or decode facial expressions and emotions and to be able to use appropriate facial expressions that will reinforce his verbal message. Facial expressions are really best learned at home through real-life experiences, within the family setting.

Home Activities

- **At home and in the community, you can talk about how we look when we are happy or sad. You can comment, "You look happy today because you're getting a new bike," or "Bobby looks sad today because his dog is sick."**
- **Use cartoon-like smiley and sad faces to stimulate discussion about when we feel happy, sad, and**

angry, and about how we look. These often come in packs of stickers, or you can use photographs or draw cartoons. Talk about when you would make that kind of face; what situations would evoke that kind of feeling.

■ **You can practice making different kinds of faces in the mirror and comment on them. Again, talk about the situations that would make you look like that face.**

Some pragmatic skills are basic to conversation and to functioning well at home, in school, and in the community, and can be learned by most children with Down syndrome. Other pragmatic skills are more advanced, and will probably only be mastered by older children and adults who function independently and at more sophisticated cognitive levels. Pragmatics is learned through interaction and experience. Your child's pragmatic skills can continue to grow throughout adulthood. Every new experience will enhance pragmatic skills. The following pragmatic skills may be more difficult for children with Down syndrome, but are worthwhile to work on; for each area, the basic and more advanced levels of the skill are discussed.

There are many pragmatic skills that your child needs to learn to be successful in conversation. But, beyond this, for all people, the speaker and listener—the communication partners—must enjoy communicating together. One of the goals of improving pragmatic skills is to make communicating fun so that your child will be motivated to communicate. So, the more practice your child gets, the better he will be at communicating and the more positive he will feel about his ability to communicate.

Conversational Skills. Conversational skills are skills that enable us to participate in conversations both as a speaker and listener. Some of the basic conversational skills, such as turn-taking, are learned even before children begin to speak. Other more advanced conversational skills, such as initiating the conversation; responding; keeping a conversation going and terminating a conversation; and knowing when to pause, how to interrupt, and how to provide feedback to the speaker, are skills that are generally learned over time through experience. They are all explained in this section.

One of the basic conversational skills, called simply "conversational manners," is knowing when you can interrupt, when not to interrupt, and how to interrupt either when it is not your turn in the conversation or when you are not part of the conversation. Role playing, and commenting during real situations (be sure it is not a situation that will embarrass your child), are the best ways to teach your child conversational manners. As more children with Down syndrome are integrated in their schools and communities, it appears that, although they may interrupt the teacher, take inappropriate turns, or ask inappropriate questions at the beginning of the school year, they usually eliminate these conversational behaviors after a few months. The natural consequences of teachers and other students saying "Don't interrupt; it's not your turn now" modifies the behavior. Experience and practice are the best teachers for conversational manners.

Stylistic Variations. Stylistic variations is the term used to describe a person's skill in adapting his communication to his audience and the situation. It is a common, yet hardly noticed, skill people use to adapt their communication to their environment. Using this skill means that we modify how we talk to people, not necessarily what we actually say. As children grow, they learn a variety of different rules or formats to use when talking with people in different social roles. This might include knowing how to use polite, formal, and colloquial language. It might involve knowing how to talk to a two-year-old cousin, a peer, a teacher, or the minister in different ways, and understanding what is appropriate for each situation. This is difficult to learn because there are so many possible permutations and different situations. Children with Down syndrome benefit from extra help and practice in this area.

Parents are usually the best teachers of this skill, and it is best taught prior to when the skill will be needed or as the situation presents itself. One of the most effective ways to teach stylistic variation is through role playing.

Home Activities

- **The practice should be done in the most "natural" setting possible. That is, the practice should closely imitate real-life situations. Set up the situation clearly, and use props and costumes to make the role playing as realistic as possible. For example, if you want your child to practice going to a friend's house for a pajama party, have him pack his pajamas, bring his radio, and take clothes for the next morning. Then set up a part of the room that is "your friend's house" and play out various scenarios to practice what is appropriate communication and what is not appropriate. For example, how do you ask your friend's mother for a soda, or what would be appropriate to say if your friend's younger brother is annoying you?**

- **Use verbal coaching or provide specific instructions to help your child give appropriate responses during the play or role playing. You might whisper in his ear to provide suggestions, such as "talk softly" or "call him Reverend Brown." Don't assume that your child is going to figure out the rules; teach your child the rules of conversation. Role play how to act at the family wedding or the dance recital, and coach your child to help him learn the communication skills needed for the situation. Then comment on and praise his successes so that he knows that he has mastered the skills needed for the situation. "You spoke so nicely to the priest" or "You used your quiet voice and were so polite when you told Aunt Kathy how pretty she looked in her new dress." If you can find a book about a similar situation, read the book together and talk about it. Practice is needed, and experience is very important in teaching this skill.**

Presuppositions. Presuppositions are the background information you assume your listener already knows without your telling him or her. Presuppositions require being able to place yourself in your listener's position. What does your listener know? What do you need to tell him? What will be familiar or unfamiliar to him? For example, if a friend asks you where is the best place to buy a new video, will he know where the store is located if you only name the store? Do you need to give directions?

Young children have difficulty with presuppositions because they are egocentric. A child will talk about his friend, Jeffrey, assuming that you know him. He will not stop to explain that Jeffrey is a friend from school. Parents can stop their child and ask, "Who is Jeffrey? I don't know him." This helps teach the child to explain what the listener needs to know. Children with Down syndrome have difficulty with presuppositions, and need more practice, coaching, and reminders to learn about what the listener needs to know. This important skill continues to develop throughout childhood and can continue to develop into adulthood.

Turn-Taking. Early development in turn-taking is discussed in the beginning chapters. But, turn-taking is also one of the important skills required in conversations for older children. Children with Down syndrome often have very short conversations. They will respond to your questions, but won't ask you any questions to keep the conversation going. They won't continue to take turns to keep the conversation active. Conversational length may also be related to topicalization (discussed below) and to vocabulary (semantic), grammatical (syntax), and verbal skills, but turn-taking skills play a role in the tendency toward short conversations. You can help your child build up to longer conversations at home, and can also help practice and reinforce those longer conversations. Often, turn-taking and topicalization must be practiced together because they are so intertwined. When you take your turn, you need to know how to continue with the topic and to stay on topic in order to keep the conversation going.

Home Activities

- **Pick a topic that you know your child will be interested in, like an upcoming trip to the baseball game. Use a visual cue, like a baseball or balloon, to show whose turn it is and to help keep the conversation going. The person who starts the conversation holds a balloon. When he finishes, he passes the balloon to the next speaker. This activity can involve two people or even a small group. Don't make the group too large, however, or your child may get bored or distracted waiting for his turn. The balloon is passed back and forth and the last speaker gets to keep the balloon. This game may motivate your child and provide practice in longer conversations. This is an exercise in turn-taking and topicalization.**

- **Play movie director, and have your children "act" out roles with dialogue that requires taking turns (write out the dialogue at first or use photos; later try to progress to improvised dialogue). Get a blackboard or a movie board, and a baseball cap or beret for the "director" as props to make this activity more fun and realistic. Cue cards may also be used to provide suggestions for your child on what to say and to emphasize that each "actor" must wait for his turn to speak. Or have a sibling play movie director and point to the person who needs to talk.**

Topicalization. Topics are the material on which conversations are based; they are the subject of conversations. It is important to learn how to choose a topic for a conversation, how to introduce a topic, how to maintain a topic, how to stay on a topic, and how to change a topic.

Maintaining a topic and staying on topic are two skills that are often difficult for children with Down syndrome. This may result from mental retardation as well as a lack of conversational experience. When you have difficulty maintaining a topic, conversations are short because you don't know what else to say about the topic. And, when you have difficulty staying on topic, your conver-

sation may seem rambling, and you may lose the interest of your listener. Much progress, however, has been made in improving topicalization skills in children with Down syndrome. Increased vocabulary and conversational skills that result from enriched experiences are probably some of the main reasons that current generations of children with Down syndrome are so much more advanced in their use of language and in their conversational ability. Former generations of children with Down syndrome, when institutionalized, didn't have these types of language or life experiences. Parents, grandparents, siblings, and the stimulation of family and community life have made a tremendous difference in the quality of language and conversational ability of children and adults with Down syndrome.

Home Activities

■ When you work with young children on categories, you are actually working on "topic" categories. Practice with older children can center on what goes with different topics. For example, if we are going to tell Aunt Sue about your new ping pong table, what would she want to know? If you want to talk about your trip to the aquarium, what could you tell your dad? What did you see? How did you get there?

- Make a gameboard with different topics on the board, such as "I got a new dress" or "We won the baseball game." Use a spinner and a gamepiece. Whatever space you land on, you have to say three things about that topic. When your child can do three, up the ante to five. Use cues, like "What else could you tell Aunt Sue about your new dress?" or "What kind of fish did you see at the aquarium?"

- Words that you associate together are part of the same topic, so association games help children learn more about topics. Games such as *Password*, *Scatter-gories*, or *Pictionary* are appropriate for working on categories and topics.

- You can also talk about topics that interest your child. For example, "if we want to talk about the baseball game, what are all the things we can talk about? We can talk about the stadium, the players, what we ate at the game, and what happened in each inning."

- Language experience activities are excellent for working on the skills needed for maintaining topics. In a language experience activity, the language is combined directly with the activity. For example, going to the supermarket is actually a rich language experience. Here is what you do: In advance, you might talk about going to the supermarket, what you *will* do, who you *will* see. Then as you are going through the supermarket, talk about what you *are* doing. Take photographs. Later, using the photographs to guide the conversation, talk about what you *did*, who you *saw*, what you *bought*, or how you carried the groceries home. You might write a story about the trip to the supermarket, using the photographs to illustrate. This provides a detailed exploration of a specific topic, and can be duplicated for other activities like baking cookies, preparing for a birthday party, or going to the circus or the ice show.

- Create books following a language experience activity. Generally, children love to read and re-read personalized books about their experiences. This helps give them "material" to talk about. Ask them questions about the book that can't be answered with just "yes," "no," or one word, such as, "What did we do at the supermarket?" Ask questions about experiences your child has had. "What did you do at Jennifer's birthday party?" Coach your child to help him stay on topic. Ask him questions like "What did you eat? Who did you see? What games did you play? What gifts did Jennifer get?"

■ Practice staying on a topic. Practice routines with your child through role playing. For example, discuss going to McDonald's with a friend, and point out what is and is not on the topic. Use props to make the situation more realistic, such as a McDonalds food box, placemat, and tray. Try to work with your child in private, but be discreet when correcting your child in public. Practice the skill, but also maintain your sense of humor. Don't expect perfection; sometimes, every child's comments are off the topic, but may be delightful comments on life. Speech-language therapy, discussed in Chapter 10, can also help improve this skill.

■ Give your child with Down syndrome visual reminders, such as photographs of a trip, to help him gain practice in lengthening the conversation. For example, talk about Disney World using photographs. Or use sequential photographs or slides of an everyday activity such as food shopping. Each person uses one photo in the sequence to talk about what is happening in the picture. Then it is the next person's turn. Take detailed photos; for example, stopping at a red light, getting the shopping cart, buying milk and eggs, and checking out. Compare the conversation you would have with your child without the photographs, and then with them. The second conversation should be longer. Talk about how each of these pictures is "on topic."

Requests. The ability to make and respond to requests appropriately is an important skill that helps ensure that our environment will meet our needs. This skill is generally learned as part of daily life, but you can help enhance and reinforce it. Comment on your child's requests when he uses them. For example, "You want more cheese. Sure, I can give you some more" or "You asked to watch the cartoons very nicely. I'll turn the TV on for you."

There are different types of requests that children with Down syndrome need to learn. Imperative ellipsis requests, or requests that name what is wanted without using a verb, are usually mastered earliest, and may be produced using Total Communication, as well as speech. For example, "more juice" is an imperative ellipsis that is learned very early in language development, often first by signing. Imperatives, such as "Give me the ball," are usually mastered by children with Down syndrome quite early. Modeling and imitation with expansion (discussed in Chapter 6) can be used to teach the different request forms.

Home Activities

- **Explicit needs and wants requests, such as "I want a drink" or "I need my coat," can be taught through pattern practice as follows:**
  > **Parent first models, "I want more cheese" or "I want my coat."**
  > **Child imitates.**
  > **Parent: "What do you want?"**
  > **Child: "More cheese."**
  > **Parent: "*I want* (emphasize) more cheese. What do you want?"**
  > **Child: "I want more cheese."**
- **Requests can be taught as a part of routines or scripts. Then it will seem natural and familiar to your child to use the request when the situation occurs. Permission requests, such as "May I go to Freddy's house to play?" can also be taught effectively through role playing and script practice.**
- **Practicing requests can also be a very good way to encourage (and demand) your child to speak in complete sentences or phrases. Children with Down syndrome tend to leave out needed elements of sen-**

tences, reducing a request like, "May I have more juice, please" to "Juice." As much as humanly possible in your life, try to insist on complete sentences or phrases when your child makes requests. One method is simply not to respond until your child makes a request with a full sentence. Another is to cue your child with a sign.

Clarification and Repairs. Clarification and repairs are two skills that go together. Clarification is asking for more information, clearing up a misunderstanding. The listener may ask for clarification ("What did you say?"), for specification ("Can you tell me what you mean?"), or for confirmation ("Is this what you are saying?"). Repairs is the ability to recognize when a communication breakdown has occurred, understand what caused the breakdown, and provide the information needed to "repair" the misunderstanding. Here are three examples of the use of clarification and repairs:

Speaker 1: Let's build a house. Bring me a big block.
Listener: There are lots of big blocks. Do you want a square block or a triangle?
Speaker: Gimme a square block.

Speaker 2: I need four quarters to be able to go to the movies.
Listener: I only have a dollar bill. Wait a minute; do you need the quarters for the bus or for the movie?
Speaker: For the bus. In the movie, they can give you change.

Speaker 3: We need to have a snack now. I'm hungry.
Listener: OK, here's some peanut butter and bread.
Speaker: I hate peanut butter
Listener: OK, how was I supposed to know that? What do you want for a snack? Do you want a graham cracker and jelly?

Initially, there was a misunderstanding between the speaker and listener in each case. In order to "repair" the misunderstanding, the speaker or the listener had to figure out what the misunderstanding was and ask for information to "clarify" what was intended.

Clarification and repairs are complex skills that are difficult for typically developing children and are especially difficult for children with Down syndrome. Practice is needed to learn how to ask for clarification and how to make repairs. This is usually worked on by your child's SLP. Home practice can help reinforce the skills.

Home Activities

■ **You can provide practice in learning these skills by asking for clarification and then helping your child make repairs so that his message is understood. This will help your child learn to respond to clarifications for repair. How do you help him learn to ask for clarification—to figure out what he doesn't understand and ask for the information? Try giving him instructions that are vague. For example, "bring me that thing." When he looks confused, ask him "What do you need to know? Ask me what thing I want." Provide models and examples, and teach him what kinds of information he needs to ask. For example, "Do I want the telephone?" Name objects that are visible that you might be asking for.**

■ **Say, "Bring me the bag" when there are three bags standing in the corner. Ask your child, "How do you know which bag I want you to bring? Ask me, 'Which bag do you want?'"**

■ **Play *Twister* but only give part of the needed information, such as "Step on the circle." Prompt your child to ask, "Which circle?" or "What color is the circle?" to repair the communication.**

Auditory Skills

There are many important skills that enable us to receive messages. One of the most important areas is auditory skills. Auditory skills for infants and toddlers are discussed in Chapters 3 and 4. This section will discuss auditory skills in older children through the elementary school years.

Auditory skills affect how your child receives, remembers, discriminates, organizes, and processes information that he hears. Children with Down syndrome usually have strengths in the area of visual skills, but are relatively weak in auditory processing. Thus, although it is important to strengthen auditory skills, it is also wise whenever possible to combine auditory stimuli with visual cues. For example, say, "Bring me your black sneakers and red socks," while pointing to the living room where your child left the sneakers. If your child can see and hear the stimuli, he will be better able to respond.

Auditory skills children with Down syndrome may have difficulty with include:

- Following long directions that are given verbally (auditory processing);
- Remembering things they hear (auditory memory);
- Comprehending messages they hear (auditory perception);
- Focusing on the message when there is noise around (auditory figure-ground);
- Differentiating speech from environmental sounds (auditory discrimination); or
- Listening to and sequencing sounds (often seen as reversals in sound production; discussed in Chapter 8).

As a result, it is harder for them to process speech alone than it is to process speech plus a visual or other cue.

Home Activities

■ **Make a specific sound and show your child how that specific sound looks (you can even use a mirror). Have a small card with the sound written on it, such as /f/. Read a list of familiar words, like "fun," "fish," "soap," "pool," and "fit." Your child has to raise the card every time he hears the /f/ sound. In the beginning, give mostly words beginning with /f/. Then, vary the sounds so that he has to listen longer and harder to hear the target sound. You can** make a check mark every time he learns the sound, and give him a reward when he hears ten sounds.

- Once your child is able to identify the sound at the beginning of a word, play the train game. There are three train cars; each has a slit in the front to insert a card. On each card is a picture; take turns with your child naming the object and then put it in the correct train car, depending on whether the target sound is at the *beginning*, in the *middle*, or at the *end* of the word.

- If you can, play several different musical instruments; let your child see the instrument and hear how it sounds. Then, ask your child to close his eyes, or put on a blindfold, listen for the sound, and tell you which musical instrument was played. Variations are to have your child point to the instrument that was played, or to point to a picture of the instrument. In the beginning, use instruments that sound very different, such as a drum and a violin; when your child masters the skill, you can use instruments that sound similar.

- Talk about the sounds that things make, such as airplanes, vacuum cleaners, animals, church bells, and water dripping out of a faucet. Listen to the sounds with your child while you both look at the object. Then, try listening with your eyes closed and concentrating on the sounds themselves. Tape record, or make the sounds one at a time, and then have your child identify them.

- Teach your child about rhyming words. Then, play rhyming baseball. Draw a baseball field gameboard on oak tag, or play this game outside on a baseball field or a small-scale chalk-drawn baseball field. Walk the bases; each base has a word on it and you have to think of rhyming words. One word is a single; four rhyming words scores a home run. You can play this with teams.

Auditory Memory is the ability to retain and recall information that we hear. Children with Down syndrome usually find it easier to remember material that is meaningful, familiar, shorter in length, and less abstract. They are best at retaining information drawn directly from their life.

- **Play the picnic game. One person says, "I am going on a picnic, and I'm taking hot dogs." The second person says, "I am going on a picnic and I'm taking hot dogs and soda." Each person adds one item to the list. To help your child in the beginning, use objects, photos, or picture cards to help him remember what was said before. Use visual cues to help reinforce auditory material.**

- **Songs, jingles, and rhythm all help memory. When your child needs to remember a string of words, make them into a song, or give them a rhythm like a football cheer. For example, the "Alphabet Song" helps children remember the letters of the alphabet.**

- **Teach your child how to best remember items. Chunking is a technique that helps memory. Put items into categories, inserting the word "and" in between categories. If you want your child to remember to buy oranges, Cheerios, Rice Krispies, milk, apples, and coffee at the store, teach him to remember the items as: milk and coffee (drinks), apples and oranges (fruits), and Cheerios and Rice Krispies (cereals). Chunking the items helps to remember them.**

- **Use short rhymes to help your child increase auditory memory skills. For example, "*Buy* the lemon *pie, go* see the *show.*" Say them with exaggerated rhythm in the beginning to help your child learn the skill.**

- **Play a following directions game. Take turns with your child. Tell him to go to the door, turn around, walk three steps, and close the door. Begin with only two instructions. Songs that involve sequences are also good for practice. For example, "Jump down, turn around and pick a bale of cotton" or "This old man."**

- **Barrier games, as described in the Pragmatics section of Chapter 10, are also good for practicing auditory memory. Give each child three different colored or shaped plastic chips. Describe which one should be first, second, and third and in what pattern. Remove the barrier and see if your child was able to follow the instructions. In the beginning, keep the commands very short.**

Auditory perception is the ability to receive and comprehend words and concepts through hearing. Generally, messages through the auditory channel only are more difficult for children with Down syndrome to process than are multi-sensory, or hearing plus visual cue, messages. They need practice in becoming good listeners. Working on this skill is important, but also try, whenever possible, to provide other environmental cues to help your child understand the message.

Home Activities

- **Listening games such as Simon Says provide excellent practice in auditory perception. This game is more fun played with groups, but watch to see whether your child is looking and doing what the other children are doing, rather than just listening. You can cue your child by repeating the instruction, or just the important words, such as "on knees."**

- **Try cookie decorating to provide practice in following auditory instructions. Or give simple recipes verbally one step at a time.**

- **Read or make up a story about several animals to a small group of children, such as "The Animal Band is Going to Toon Town." Give each child the name of one of the animals and teach him how to make the sound of that animal. Whenever he hears the name of "his" animal in the story, he has to stand up and make "his" animal sound.**

Auditory figure-ground skills refers to the ability to hear a message even though there is background noise. It is the ability to separate the important sounds from the background sounds.

Children with Down syndrome are sometimes distracted by background noise in the classroom, a restaurant, or at home, and may find it difficult to focus on speech when there is extraneous noise. You can often build up a tolerance to noise by working on focusing when there is noise, keeping the message loud and the background noise soft. You may have to simulate the background noise on a tape recorder in order to enable you to control the volume. Vary the noise and the activity; this is the best way to work on auditory figure-ground skills at home. You may want to have your child wear a Mickey Mouse Hat and call the ears his "listening ears." Often, if you prepare your child to listen, it will be easier for him to block out noise and listen for the message. Try using a word that cues your child that it is time to listen carefully, such as "ear ready." You could also try to call your child by name before he needs to listen "hard" so that he will be able to consciously block out background noise. Other approaches are providing visual cues, such as pointing to your ear to signal it is time to listen, reducing background noise, and making sure that your child always sits in the front of the room where there will be fewer sound distractions.

Advanced Language Skills

Certain language skills are more advanced, but can be mastered by many children with Down syndrome. These language skills are particularly useful for advanced schoolwork, including full inclusion in late elementary school grades and higher. This section reviews the advanced language skills.

Conversational Skills

In the discussion of pragmatics above, basic conversational skills were addressed. There are several more sophisticated conversational skills.

Idioms, or the use of figures of speech like "raining cats and dogs," are difficult for children with Down syndrome because they are abstract and often don't mean what the words say. There are usually books of idioms in the library in the section on learning English as a second language, or you can teach the idioms that appear in real life by making them into games.

- Help your child learn more about idioms by drawing pictures or using photographs. For example, a photograph of rain and a drawing of cats and dogs raining would be both useful and humorous. Other idioms that are fun to play with include "bite off more than you can chew," "the cat's got your tongue," "your eyes are bigger than your stomach," "the apple of your eye." Make the idiom practice into a funny time, and enjoy exploring the meaning of the idioms.

Ability to Follow Longer, More Complex Directions is a necessary skill for success if your child is included in upper elementary school grades. This is a more advanced skill because it involves the ability to retrieve what is stored in auditory memory and act on it.

- Games that involve following instructions are helpful. Some examples are "Red Light - Green Light," "Take a Giant Step."
- Board games such as *CandyLand* and *Chutes and Ladders* that involve following instructions are good beginning choices. Games for older children such as *Life*, *Sorry*, and card games such as *Go Fish*, *Old Maid*, and *UNO* may be helpful and enjoyable as well. *Twister* is another good choice for learning to follow instructions.

Children with Down syndrome often have difficulty as the instructions become longer and more complex. A typical school instruction may be very long and complex, such as, "Fold your paper in half, number from 1-10 on the left and from 11-20 on the right. Put your name and today's date in the upper left hand corner and raise your hand when you have finished." How can you help your child learn to follow more complex instructions? Work up to complex instructions slowly and base the instructions on individual concepts that your child already knows. For example, use the terms "swivel chair" and "large desk" only when you know that your child knows the concepts, chair, swivel, large, desk, and front. Only then should you say, "Can you move the swivel chair over to the large desk in the front of the room?" Following instructions can be incorporated into daily life. Some suggestions are:

- Use household tasks to practice following instructions. For example, when your child is helping you clean the counter, say "Would you get me the sponge and the cleanser?"
- Use recipes to help your child learn to follow instructions. Have him practice following instructions not only in assembling the ingredients, but also in the steps involved in the recipe. Say, "pour in two cups of milk" or "mix the flour and baking soda together." Cooking is an ideal activity, because it is practical, helps practice many skills, and includes a bonus—something you can eat when you finish.
- Crafts projects such as making a felt wreath, a recipe box, or a flowered hat offer practice in following instructions.

Some skills useful in the classroom may actually involve the combination of several communication skills: for example, the ability to listen to and follow instructions (receptive language and auditory processing); the ability to encode messages, explain actions, and express feelings (expressive language); and the ability to use language to interact with others, take turns, and share (pragmatics).

How can you help your child master and practice the more advanced communication skills needed in school? Many of the necessary skills have been mastered at an earlier stage, but just have to be adapted to the rules of the school. For example, your child knows about turn-taking; now he needs to learn that to take a turn in school, he needs to raise his hand. In the toddler and pre-school years, you worked on categories with your child; now, what goes into a category can be the basis for practice about topics or subject matter. For example, if your child needs to give a report about his pet, ask him what he should include in the report, and ask him questions about his pet.

- Practice scripts of common situations, such as telling the teacher about a new game that Grandma brought as a present. You play the teacher and role play the situation. Coach your child. Give suggestions like "tell me how many people can play," "tell me if you keep score," or "tell me how you win." Then, reverse the roles. You be your child and tell him (the teacher) about the new game.

- Practice asking and answering questions. The game *Twenty Questions* is good for this practice. In the beginning, have the object visible and discuss the various traits, such as "It's yellow, It's long and curved, It's a fruit." Then begin to play the game. Coach your child until he is able to master the questioning skills. Then, it's fine to "think" of the answer rather than having the object visible, and to gradually reduce the amount of coaching.

Motivation for Learning Language Skills

Language and communication are part of daily life. When some skills don't come easily, there is a tendency to want your child with

Down syndrome to practice and do "homework" to learn those skills. The problem is that making language practice into homework will usually turn your child off. As much as possible, make language skill practice part of your daily activities. Use your errands such as food shopping, going to the bank, and buying gasoline as practice sessions; use a drive in the car or a walk as the basis for practice, but don't label it as language practice. Make it fun, make it spontaneous, make it part of life. Do not distinguish between language games and "real" games. *All* the games are fun and can involve your whole family. Remember, above all, that your child would like to be able to do well in language effortlessly, and that your child wants to please you. Don't make language practice hard work; try to make it hard fun.

Conclusion

Although complex, language can be learned by all children, including children with Down syndrome. With practice and through daily life experiences, they can master the many different language skills necessary for them to function well at home, in school, and in the community.

As you work with your child on the activities suggested in this chapter, remember that you do not need to turn every daily activity into a learning opportunity. It is OK to relax and just have fun sometimes. However, with minimal effort, you will be surprised at the great number of language learning opportunities that exist in everyday life, and you will be pleased with the progress your child can make.

8 | SPEECH AND INTELLIGIBILITY PROBLEMS AND HOME ACTIVITIES

The purpose of communication is to get your message across; to have people understand you. Communication has two parts: The first, discussed in Chapter 7, is language, or the ability to encode and decode understandable messages; the second, discussed in this chapter, is speech, or the ability to convey messages verbally. Both language and speech are vital to everyday life, work, and school.

Speech intelligibility—being able to convey a message clearly so that the listener can understand it—is quite important. It is very frustrating to constantly have people ask, "Can you say that again? I didn't understand you." It is even worse if your child or the people she talks to just give up in frustration.

The usual focus of professionals and parents in communication development of children with Down syndrome is on language. Sometimes speech-language pathologists (SLPs) concentrate on language and communication skills, rather than on speech skills. They may not place as much importance on speech intelligibility because they expect the child to spend most of her life around people who know her well and are accustomed to her speech. But with inclusion becoming a reality and opportunities for community interaction increasing, intelligibility of speech becomes an extremely important issue. As your child's circle of friends, acquaintances, and co-workers becomes larger, she interacts with many more people who may have difficulty in understanding her speech. She needs intelligible speech to function well in her world.

Fortunately, there are many things that you can do to help your child overcome the different speech problems affecting intelligibility. This chapter describes the speech problems that affect children with Down syndrome, and provides home activities that address the problem areas.

Speech Intelligibility Problems of Children with Down Syndrome

A variety of speech problems make it more difficult for children with Down syndrome to be understood. But if the speech problems affecting intelligibility can be identified, a great deal of knowledge can now be applied to help improve intelligibility. For example, if your child is known to have weak tongue muscles, she can do exercises to strengthen those muscles. Much has been learned about the potential of people with Down syndrome to speak intelligibly and about the therapy and educational techniques to tap that potential fully.

You may encounter professionals and non-professionals who act as if your child's intelligibility problems are "part of Down syndrome." They may say, "Of course she has difficulty in being understood; she has Down syndrome." But, your child's intelligibility problems, if any, are not exclusive to people with Down syndrome. All of the factors that might affect her intelligibility can also be found in children and adults without Down syndrome, and there is no one specific speech pattern that is characteristic of all children with Down syndrome.

Speech Problems Affecting Intelligibility

When we think of intelligibility, we usually think about the way children make the sounds. Many parents say, "If my child could only produce the sounds more clearly, people would understand him." Articulation or the ability to produce the sounds of language is an important factor in intelligibility, but there are many other factors that also need to be considered. Intelligibility is often thought of globally—as just a part of Down syndrome. Thinking about intelligibility in general terms is not helpful. It is important to address the *specific* speech, language, and conversational characteristics that influence whether your child can be understood. Table 1 summarizes these area which are discussed in detail in the sections below.

TABLE 1
FACTORS AFFECTING INTELLIGIBILITY
- Rate
- Loudness
- Fluency
- Articulation
- Phonological processes
- Tongue Thrust/Swallowing pattern
- Voice quality
- Resonance
- Nonverbal factors
- Pragmatic factors

Rate

The rate of speech, or how fast we talk, is an important factor in whether a person can be easily understood. Rate can be slow, rapid, or variable. In my experience as a speech-language pathologist, I have found that children with Down syndrome often speak rapidly or in spurts. They may start out at a comfortable rate for the listener, but often speed up as the conversation progresses. Fast or spurted rate may result in slurred or difficult-to-understand speech because there are no pauses between words, and words tend to run into each other. If your child has trouble speaking at an appropriate rate, there are a variety of activities you can try at home.

Home activities

■ **A pacing board may be used to help your child develop a more regular rhythmic pattern. Chapter 6 describes pacing boards in detail. Using a pacing board frequently helps slow down speech. If she is typically using five words, the pacing board would** have five circles or five stickers. Your child would put her finger on the first circle as she said the first word, the second circle as she said the second word, and so on. This acts as a visual reminder to speak more rhythmically.

- Lightly beat a drum as your child speaks, and have her try to match her speech rate to the drum. For example, have your child practice saying a phrase such as "Hi! How are you? I'm fine. Bye now!" to the accompaniment of a drumbeat. You can also use a metronome for this type of practice.

- Have conversations with your child in which each of you sings your words to a musical rhythm. You can use a song that your child already knows or make up a different tune. You can use slow and fast songs. For example, you and your child would sing "Good morning. I'm glad to see you. Have a good day." When your child can do this slowly and rhythmically, the "singing" can gradually be phased out.

- Talk about slow and fast speech and demonstrate slow and fast speech. Play a game in which you say sentences or read a story while your child moves a car along a toy road. When you speak slowly, she moves the car slowly. When you speed up, she should have the car speed up. When this becomes familiar, have your child repeat phrases after you, and move the car along at the speed of speech. This activity can be varied with a horse on a trail or a boat on a toy river.

- With older children who have mastered pacing but still tend to speak rapidly or in spurts sometimes, agree on a signal to unobtrusively let your child know that she is talking too fast. If she is able to monitor herself, an activity such as tapping her finger on her leg may enable her to get back in rhythm when she senses that she is talking too fast.

Loudness

To be intelligible, your child needs to speak at the appropriate volume level. When children with Down syndrome have difficulty with volume, it is usually because they are speaking too softly, rather than too loudly. Sometimes problems with volume can be traced to a physical condition. For example, a child who has fluctuating hearing loss because of recurrent ear infections may have trouble monitoring her own volume. Or a child with low muscle tone may not have the breath support to speak loudly. If your child has difficulties with volume, the first step is therefore to consult an otolaryngologist (ENT)—a physician who specializes in the diagnosis and treatment of conditions in the ear, nose, and throat. If there is a problem such as lack of sufficient breath to produce adequate loudness, that must be addressed by your child's doctor and speech pathologist.

Some children speak very loudly or even scream. It is very important to teach children not to shout or scream constantly because this can result in damage to the vocal mechanism. This problem is not unique to children with Down syndrome; many typically developing children shout to the point of needing voice therapy.

Usually, when children with Down syndrome have chronic low speech volume, there is no underlying physical cause. Low volume may be related to lack of confidence, lack of experience, or overcompensation for trying not to shout. In addition, your child's volume may be inconsistent, or she may not modulate her volume appropriately to the environment. Loudness needs to match the size of the room, whether the conversation is outdoors or indoors, and the number of communication partners, as well as their ages and abilities. For example, it is appropriate to speak loudly or shout when playing dodge ball on the playground with other children, but not at the movies. So, what your child may really need to learn is *when* to be loud and when to use a quiet voice, and this is best taught at home and in the community in real-life situations. At home, you can let your child know that you are having difficulty hearing her and that she needs to speak more loudly. You can let your child know that you are on the phone and she needs to use a soft voice. You can also discuss and practice different situations. Practice may be all that is needed to increase or decrease the loudness of the voice. Failing to use appropriate volume is a problem many "typically developing" children experience. If you have found a method for helping your other children learn when to be loud and when to be soft, it will likely work for your child with Down syndrome.

Home activities

- **Talk about loud and soft voices. Label voices as your "inside" and "outside" voices. Practice using a loud voice (in a tunnel so you can hear the echo) and a soft voice (from a whisper to a quiet voice).**

- **Comment on loud and soft noises in the environment. For example, when you hear the lion at the zoo, comment on the loud roar. Listen to quiet sounds in the environment, such as water dripping and birds chirping, and comment on them.**

- **Talk about places where you need to use a soft voice, such as school or church, and places where you can use a loud voice, such as baseball or hockey games or on a roller coaster. This is most helpful if you can talk about loudness/softness immediately before your child will encounter the situation.**

- **Read books about whispering and loud and soft sounds. *Mr. Brown Can Moo, Can You?* by Dr. Seuss, *Noisy Nora* by Rosemary Wells, *SHHH!* by Suzy Kline, *Noisemakers* by Judith Caseley, and *Helen and The Great Quiet* by Rick Fitzgerald are some favorite books for talking about volume.**

- **Play games where your child has to use a loud or soft voice or a whisper. "Telephone" is a good game to use, but remember to keep the messages short. Several children stand in a line. The first child whispers a message in the ear of the next child in line, and so on down the line. The last child has to**

repeat the message he or she heard and compare it to the message the first child sent.

■ **When your child has learned how to control volume, but doesn't remember to do so, use a sign at home as a reminder, such as a cartoon that shows Fred Flintstone holding his hand behind his ear and saying "Speak Up" or Fred Flintstone holding his finger on his lips as in "Sh-h-h." Or when away from home, agree on a signal, such as a thumbs up for speak up and closing and opening your hand for speak more softly.**

Fluency

Fluency refers to the smoothness of speech—how easily one sound flows into the next sound, one syllable flows into the next syllable, and one word flows into the next word. Problems with fluency are sometimes referred to as stuttering. Fluency problems in children with Down syndrome have not been sufficiently studied to date. But it appears that more parents than ever before are noticing problems with fluency in their children with Down syndrome. The problem is usually first noticed at ten to thirteen years of age, and it tends to occur in children and adolescents who have a high level of language ability and expressive output. Your child may have repetitions (clonic blocks) or periods of silence in which she seems to be struggling to emit a sound (tonic blocks). There is no conclusive data to determine whether fluency problems in children with Down syndrome are related to a neurological or cognitive problem or to a respiratory, motor, or airflow problem. Parents have been contacting professionals because many adolescents are no longer receiving SLP services when the fluency difficulty is noticed. Fluency problems often occur together with rate problems; children who speak rapidly may also demonstrate difficulties in fluency.

If your child has fluency problems, it is important not to draw attention to them. This can only increase tension in her breathing mechanism and articulators (discussed below) and make fluent speech more difficult. Drawing attention to fluency problems may also make your child avoid speaking. In general, you should maintain eye contact, be very patient, and listen to what your child is saying. Don't fill in the words that are giving your child difficulty and don't tell her to slow down. Let your child know that you will continue to listen to her until she is finished. Fluency problems are complex and need to be treated by a professional. A speech-language pathologist will best be able to help your child with fluency difficulties. He or she will suggest home activities appropriate to the specific type of fluency problems your child has. Evaluation of fluency problems and treatment of fluency problems are discussed in later chapters.

Articulation

In the English language, there are forty-three distinct speech sounds, or *phonemes.* These include all the vowel and consonant sounds used in the language, such as /p/, /k/, /f/, and /e/. These speech sounds are produced by the process of articulation—that is, by moving the *articulators:* the lips, tongue, upper and lower jaw, hard and soft palate, alveolar ridge (the gum ridge behind the upper teeth), and teeth. Articulation is a complex process, and requires that a child know how to:

- position her articulators in proper relation to each other to produce a given sound (place of production);

- modify her breath stream appropriately as the sound is produced (manner of production); and
- either vibrate the vocal cords or don't vibrate them, as appropriate (voicing).

Table 2 shows how different sounds in the English language are produced using different places of production, manners of production, and voicing.

TABLE 2

PLACE OF PRODUCTION FOR SOUNDS OF ENGLISH

PLACE OF PRODUCTION	SOUNDS PRODUCED
Upper and Lower Lip:	P, B, W, M, WH
Lower Lip and Upper Teeth:	F, V
Tongue Between Teeth:	TH (*TH*IS), TH (*TH*IN)
Tongue Tip Behing Upper Teeth:	T, D, L, N
Tongue Blade and Alveolar Ridge:	S, Z
Tongue and Palate:	SH, ZH (MEASURE), CH, J
Front Palate:	Y
Central Palate:	R
Velum (Soft Palate):	K, G, NG
Glottis (Voice Box):	H

MANNER OF PRODUCTION FOR SOUNDS OF ENGLISH

MANNER OF PRODUCTION	SOUNDS PRODUCED
PLOSIVES:	
Sounds are made by stopping the air and releasing it with a little explosion	Plosive Sounds are P, B, T, D, K, G
FRICATIVES:	
Sounds are made by sending the air through partially closed articulators	Fricative Sounds are S, Z, F, V, SH, ZH, TH (*TH*IN), TH (*TH*IS)

AFFRICATES:

Sounds are combinations of a Plosive and a Fricative sound

Affricate Sounds are CH (*CH*IP), J (*J*UD*GE*)

GLIDES:

The Glide Sound is R

LATERAL SOUNDS:

The Lateral Sound is L

NASALS:

Sounds where the breath stream is send out through the nasal cavity

Nasal Sounds are M, N, NG (RI*NG*)

VOICING OF ENGLISH LANGUAGE SOUNDS

—ALL VOWEL SOUNDS ARE VOICED (involve vibration of the vocal cords).

—CONSONANT SOUNDS MAY BE VOICED OR UNVOICED (SOMETIMES CALLED VOICELESS).

- UNVOICED SOUNDS ARE: P, T, K, F, S, TH (*TH*IN), SH, CH
- VOICED SOUNDS ARE: B, D, G, Z, TH (*TH*IS), ZH, J, M, N, NG,L, R, V, W, Y.

How Down Syndrome Affects Articulation

Because articulation is such a complex process, it is not surprising that children with Down syndrome (and other children, as well) often have trouble producing sounds correctly. Some specific difficulties that may affect articulation in children with Down syndrome include:

- Hearing impairments or fluctuating hearing;
- Low muscle tone (hypotonicity)—flaccid or floppy muscles;
- Dysarthria—difficulty controlling movements due to damage to the central or peripheral nervous system; and
- Verbal apraxia—difficulty planning the voluntary movements needed to make speech sounds.

Hearing Impairments

Most of us learn the sounds of our language by hearing those sounds. The typically developing child will probably hear a word 2000 times or more before she uses that word in speech. Children with Down syndrome often need to hear a word even more times before they can say it. This can be difficult when a child has recurrent middle ear infections with fluctuating hearing loss—as many children with Down syndrome do. Ear infections complicate learning the sounds of the language, because your child may accurately hear the sounds at one time but not at another. She needs to hear the sounds frequently and consistently in order to learn them accurately.

As a parent, the best way you can minimize the effects of hearing problems on speech production is to seek prompt medical attention for ear infections, and to follow through on the physician's treatment plan. Sometimes when your child constantly has ear infections, it can get to the point where you feel that the ear infection is a very minor medical situation. You may feel "it's just another ear infection." But "just another ear infection" can have a major impact on hearing and can further delay speech development. For example, children who have fluctuating hearing loss may not hear the final sounds in words such as "coats," "walked," and "felt" because they are typically said more softly. Consult Chapters 2 and 3 for information that you can use to help your child develop the auditory bases of language.

Low Muscle Tone

As earlier chapters discuss, children with Down syndrome frequently have hypotonicity or low muscle tone. Muscles in the facial area, as well as in the arms, legs, and neck may be floppier, or more relaxed. When muscles in the lips, tongue, and cheeks have low tone, speech may sound imprecise, thickened, or slurred. Children might talk in shorter utterances because they are unable to sustain a breath long enough to say a whole sentence.

If your child has low muscle tone in the lips, tongue, and cheeks, her speech-language pathologist will work with her in therapy to improve her muscle tone and coordination. There are also some exercises that you can use with your child in the Home Activities section below.

Dysarthria

The ability to produce speech sounds is also affected by the development and maturation of the nerves and muscles. Some children with Down syndrome have gaps in neurological develop-ment that make it harder to control and coordinate the complex movements needed for speech. For example, the words "*spl*ash" and "*spr*inkle" require complex movements. The difficulty may be because certain infant reflexes that usually disappear in early childhood persist. It is believed that these "primitive" reflexes, such as the rooting reflex that makes a child open her mouth when an object comes near, interfere with higher levels of neurological development. Likewise, the inability to move one part of the oral mechanism such as the tongue or lips without moving the whole body can also hinder development.

When a child has dysarthria, she usually has difficulties with all movements of the mouth and face. Not only does she have trouble articulating speech sounds, but she also has trouble chewing and swallowing. She may also have difficulty with other aspects of speech discussed elsewhere in this chapter, including voice, resonance, and fluency.

Children who have dysarthria are very consistent in the types of speech problems they have. For example, they may always mispronounce their name in the same way, or always run out of breath after saying three words. Generally, if the muscles can per-form a task, they will work in approximately the same way each time, but if the muscles have difficulty in performing a task, they will have consistent difficulty. Usually the difficulty is not linked to specific sounds. That is, it is not simply that a child has trouble with the /t/ sound, but that she has overall difficulties producing speech sounds.

If your child has dysarthria, the speech-language pathologist can provide an exercise program to help strengthen weak muscles. Some suggestions for activities to do at home are included at the end of this section.

Verbal Apraxia

In contrast to dysarthria, verbal apraxia is a motor programming problem, not a muscular problem. Children with apraxia, often called developmental verbal apraxia, have the physical ability to make the movements needed for speech, but have difficulty putting them into proper order. The muscles themselves are not affected, and there may be no difficulty in using the muscles for eating or swallowing.

Children who have verbal apraxia are very inconsistent. One time, a child may be able to produce her cousin's name clearly; another time, she may have great difficulty. Typically, children with apraxia also make many sound reversals in their words. They might say, "aminal" or "hopsital" or "efelant." They may be physically capable of producing all the speech sounds, but have trouble putting them in the proper sequence. When the speech-language pathologist tests for this problem, she usually asks the child to say multisyllable words such as hamburger, elephant, or hospital, or complex words such as aluminum, linoleum, or statistics. As words get longer, children with motor programming problems such as apraxia start to have difficulty. So, a child might be able to say "light," but "lightning bug" may be difficult. Or "eel" might be fine, but "electricity" will be difficult. Verbal apraxia is a complex problem that needs to be evaluated and treated by a professional. If home activities are appropriate, the speech-language pathologist will suggest the specific activities that you can do at home with your child, but these activities need to be specifically prescribed by the SLP.

Not every child with Down syndrome has all or even any of the difficulties described above. Children with Down syndrome may have articulation problems without dysarthria or apraxia; articulation problems with dysarthria; articulation problems with verbal apraxia; or articulation problems with dysarthria and verbal apraxia.

In evaluating your child's speech, the speech-language pathologist should always consider whether intelligibility problems are complicated by dysarthria or verbal apraxia. Determining which of these problems is present is important because remediation techniques for the problems are very different. For some types of dysarthria, such as hypotonicity, it is important to use muscle strengthening exercises for the lips and the tongue, cheek, and jaw muscles. For developmental verbal apraxia, or motor programming problems, it is important to use drill and repetition, with many visual-tactile cues, such as placing the SLP's fingers on your child's lips when the child is learning the /p/, /b/, or /m/ sounds, or having the child touch the throat area when learning the /k/ and /g/ sounds. The bottom line is that therapy needs to be different for the two problems if the therapy is to be effective.

Home Activities

The following activities will help to strengthen your child's muscles for articulation and promote awareness of her articulators. They will also provide practice for your child in listening to the specific sounds of speech and in producing them accurately.

Activities for Promoting Oral-Motor Strength and Coordination

1. Look in a mirror together with your child and have fun moving your lips and tongue.

- **Round your lips**
- **Blow kisses**
- **Smack your lips**
- **Smile and then pucker**

- Say /oo/ as in soup and then /ee/ as in meet
- Frown
- Open your mouth wide
- Close your mouth tightly
- Reach for the sky with your tongue (move your tongue up as if to touch your nose)
- Lick your lips (try smearing peanut butter, jelly, or ice cream on your child's lips to encourage her to lick)
- Say /mmmm/
- Yawn
- Sigh

2. Do the same activities without the mirror. Look at each other when you make the sounds and then imitate each other.

3. Blowing bubbles is an activity that children love. Siblings and grandparents can also help with this activity. For a long time, your child will not actually blow bubbles. It's the lip rounding that you're practicing first. The bubble blowing will start as your child gains additional breath control. Older children with Down syndrome can blow bubbles to delight younger siblings.

4. Whistles provide excellent practice for the lip rounding and lip compression needed for making sounds such as /p/, /b/, /m/, and /w/. When you begin practice, you will need a whistle with a large round mouthpiece. If your child cannot seal her lips around the whistle, increase the circumference of the mouthpiece. This can be done in two ways:

- Take the rod out of a foam hair curler. Stretch the foam curler over the mouthpiece of the whistle.
- Wrap a piece of sponge around the mouthpiece. Secure it around the mouthpiece.

To make practice more interesting, get a variety of intriguing types of whistles. Some that we use in our center have miniature trains circling and a whistle with a slide. We use the MORE whistle sets available from PDP Products, Hugo, Minnesota, cited in the Resources section. You can play rhythms with the whistles, take turns blowing, or simply blow long and loud. The lip compression and lip rounding practice helps strengthen the lip muscles.

5. Real or toy musical instruments may help your child with lip movements, as well as with breath control. If it's a toy, try blowing the toy instrument yourself to be sure that it is not too difficult or frustrating to blow. Consult your SLP or a music teacher to determine which instruments might be beneficial and which instruments your child might be ready for. The recorder is an instrument that many children with Down syndrome play and enjoy.

6. For the older child, design a lip and tongue Olympics. Have events such as the activities used for mirror practice above. Add higher level activities. For example:

- Hold your tongue up right behind your teeth for a count of 10.

- See how high the coach (you) can count while your child holds her tongue up.

- Round /oo/ and retract (smile) the lips alternately ten times.

- Open your mouth a little, then a little wider, and then close.

- Open and then close the mouth (increasing the number of times and increasing the speed).

- Move the tongue from one corner of the mouth to the other.

- Lick the entire perimeter of the lips (slowly and carefully).

- Touch the outside of your child's cheek; have her move her tongue to that spot on the inside of her cheek.

Award prizes for each event mastered, or use a checksheet and check off each skill mastered. When your child has completed four events, award a ribbon or a special prize such as lunch or a movie together.

7. For older children, you can design a "Make That Face" gameboard to help practice the movements. Opened manila folders make wonderful gameboards and are easy to store. Use a spinner and game pieces. On selected spaces, draw in cartoons or pictures and instructions, like "Make a kissing sound with your lips." Another variation is to put the instructions on cards and have the gameboard spaces say, "Pick a red card" or "Pick a yellow card."

8. Use a hopscotch grid on the ground. In each square, place a card listing an activity involving the tongue or lips. Wherever the stone is thrown, everyone has to do what it says.

9. Play a team game such as "Double Dare" involving activities and physical challenges. Make the activities lip and tongue movements. Here are some examples to get you started:

- Put peanut butter on the top lip only. The contestant must lick it off in a specified time.

- Put a marshmallow on a long string. Your child has to get the marshmallow into her mouth using only her tongue, teeth, and lips. Only use this activity if there is no danger that your child will swallow the string.

Additional Activities for Sound Stimulation

10. Give each sound a name. For example, /z/ is the buzzing sound or /p/ is the motorboat sound. Play with a toy that makes that sound.

11. For sound awareness, have a "sound" day. If it's /p/ day, have pizza for lunch and porterhouse steak or pork, potato, pasta, and peas for dinner. Make popcorn, or have peanuts or potato chips as a snack. Go to the park or the party store and have a treasure hunt to name as many things as you can starting with the sound. Play Nerf ping pong as a family activity, and read a *Peanuts* book together.

This activity can be adapted for older children by varying the activities. For example, go to the video store or a game arcade and play all of the games that have "p" in their titles.

The same activity can be done with any of the sounds listed earlier in this chapter. If your child is enrolled in speech therapy, stimulate the sounds currently addressed in therapy; if not, try the sounds in your child's name, sibling's names, or your last name, or sounds from other important words in her life.

12. Sometimes, older children can articulate a word accurately when it is said alone. For example, some children with Down syndrome can say the word "cake" alone, but have difficulty when that word is in a sentence like "I want more cake." One way to practice making longer and more clearly articulated sentences is through using carrier phrases such as "I want some...." and the pacing board as described in earlier chapters. Write out on cards:"cake"..."more cake"... "I want cake"... "I want more cake." Use a pacing board with 4 circles, or have your child tap out a rhythm as she says the words. Point to each circle as you say, "I want more cake."

13. If your child is having difficulty with multisyllabic words like "railroad train" or "birthday cake," try having your child practice words of similar length while she pounds lightly on a drum. For example, "pancake house," "rock and roll," and "hamburger."

14. Play a mirror imitation game. You say a word with the sound to be practiced while looking in the mirror. Your child keeps looking in the mirror and tries to say the word exactly the way you did. To keep the practice fun, make some words loud, others whispered, still others dramatic.

Phonological Processes

As young children first develop speech, most use what are called "phonological processes." These are sound simplifications or substitution patterns they discover, usually on their own, that make their speech production easier. For example, a child may say /fum/ instead of /thumb/. Or she may leave off all of the final consonant sounds in words, saying /ca/ for both /cat/ and /cap/. At the same time, she may say /po/ for /pot/ and /to/ for /top/, proving that she is capable of saying the final consonants of cat and cap. The problem is that she doesn't know when to use these sounds, not that she can't say them.

Usually, typically developing children do not use phonological processes beyond the age of five. Children with Down syndrome, however, often continue to use these simplifications much longer. Research has not pinpointed why children with Down syndrome use phonological processes longer, but has determined which processes they tend to use.

The most common phonological processes used by children with Down syndrome are:

- final consonant deletion (ba for bat)
- fronting, or making all sounds in the front of the mouth (tootie for cookie)
- backing, or making all sounds in the back of the mouth (gagi for daddy)
- weak syllable deletion (hamger for hamburger)
- consonant cluster reduction (gass for glass)

Children with Down syndrome often have all of the phonological processes listed above, but sometimes only have some. Final consonant deletion is the most frequently occurring phonological process in children with Down syndrome. This may be because final sounds are generally said more quietly. The ability to hear these sounds may be reduced in children with Down syndrome who have fluctuating hearing loss.

Your child's pattern of phonological processes will have a direct impact on the intelligibility of speech. Sound simplifications and substitutions make speech more difficult to understand, especially for people not familiar with your child's speech.

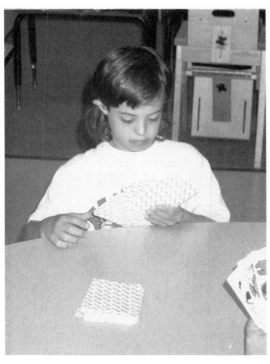

Activities for Phonological Processes

There are many different phonological processes used by children, and you need to rely on the evaluation of the SLP to identify the specific processes your child uses. Here are some home activities for the most commonly occurring processes.

Final Consonant Deletion:

1. **Play a game called "End That Word."** Show pictures of words with three sounds, but only give the first two sounds. For example, /ba/ for bat or /ta/ for tack. Your child has to say the word with the final sound emphasized, such as battt, takkk. Take turns.

2. **Play a game called "Put the Tail on the Dog."** Use cards with pictures of objects; say the word with the final sound emphasized. Discuss that the final sound on a word is like the tail on the dog; it needs to be right at the end. Say the word with the final sound attached and you get to pin the tail on the dog.

3. **Make up cards for a game like Go Fish.** First, come up with a list of pairs of words that are pronounced the same except for the final sound, such as "bat" and "bath," "fish and "fist," "pet" and "pen," and "tea" and "team." Then, make two of each word card. You and your child take turns asking, "Do you have any

bats?" The goal is to say the final sounds and to get the largest number of pairs, such as pairs of "bats" or pairs of "baths."

Fronting and Backing:

1. Talk about the fact that some sounds like /p/ and /l/ are made right in the front of the mouth and other sounds like /k/ and /g/ are made at the back of the mouth. Make a toy house with a front door and a back door. Practice making a front sound whenever you open the front door and a back sound whenever you open the back door. Use a mirror to see the front sounds and touch your throat area to feel the back sounds.

Weak Syllable Deletion:

1. The most effective home activity for weak syllable deletion is using a drum or pacing board to pound out, count out, or touch the number of syllables. For example, ham-bur-ger, base-ball-bat. Another possibility is to "sing" the word in a three-part rhythm, ham-bur-ger. You might want to emphasize the syllable that is usually omitted or say it louder.

Consonant Cluster Reduction:

1. When your child omits one consonant in the cluster, such as "cown" for "clown," the most effective home technique is to add an "a" sound after the first consonant sound and emphasize the two sounds in practice. For example, for "clown," say, "ca-lown," "ga-lass." Sometimes, children enjoy doing a dance while practicing these clusters. For motivation, you can also make chocolate cluster candy with chocolate chips, marshmallows, and peanuts, and drop in some pieces each time your child practices a cluster sound.

Tongue Thrust/Swallowing Pattern

Many children with Down syndrome have difficulty with tongue thrust—that is, with the tongue protruding and thrusting out of the mouth during eating, speaking, and other times. You may have been told that your child has a deviate swallow or a reverse swallow or myofunctional problems or difficulties in orofacial myology. These terms all describe the same pattern of tongue thrust.

A speech symptom that often accompanies tongue thrust is the substitution of /th/ for /s/—for example, saying /thun/ for /sun/. This is sometimes referred to as an interdental lisp.

A tongue thrusting pattern can be diagnosed by the speech-language pathologist. It is then usually treated together by an orthodontist and speech-language pathologist. The orthodontist can use braces to improve the tooth alignment, but this will only change the form in the oral cavity. At the same time, the speech-language pathologist can use exercises to correct any imbalance between the strength of the muscles of the lips, tongue, and jaw, thus changing the function as well. Braces or strengthening exercises alone are usually not enough. If only braces are used, the tongue will again begin to exert outward pressure against the teeth as soon as the braces are removed. If only exercises are used, the mouth size and shape may still lead to tongue thrusting.

Some parents have considered facial reconstructive surgery, specifically tongue reduction surgery, to improve their child's speech. In Israel, tongue reduction surgery is routinely performed for children with Down syndrome before the age of two years. Some research has found that this can improve a child's ability to keep her tongue inside her mouth. Based on current research findings, however, it does not appear that tongue reduction surgery improves speech or articulation. Although tongue reduction surgery reduces the size of the tongue, it does not affect its function. In my experience, the strength and mobility of the tongue muscles have the biggest impact on a child's speech, not the size of the tongue.

Home Activities

Any activity in the preceding sections that strengthens the tongue muscles and the lip muscles will help your child keep her tongue in her mouth, and keep her lips closed. There are specific exercise programs that accompany myofunctional therapy, but those must be prescribed by a professional depending on your child's specific myofunctional pattern. These exercises can include tongue touching and lip pursing.

Voice Quality and Resonance

Your child's voice quality can affect the intelligibility of her speech. When listening to your child speak, if people must focus on her voice, it will be more difficult for them to focus on her message. Many children with Down syndrome who have allergies have a hoarse voice. A breathy or husky voice is also common in many children, but the cause has not been well researched.

Resonance—the tonal quality of speech—is another factor that may influence whether the message can be understood. When someone sounds like they have a cold or are all stuffed up, you are hearing the quality of vocal resonance. In the English language, all sounds except /m/, /n/, and /ng/ are resonated in the oral cavity (mouth), not the nasal cavity. For a child to have normal resonance, she needs a clear nasal pathway for nasal sounds like /m/, /n/, and /ng/ and adequate muscle function to close off the nasal passage when the air should be resonating in the mouth for sounds like /b/ and /d/.

Many children with Down syndrome have resonance problems. The most common are *hyponasality,* or decreased nasal resonance, and *hypernasality,* or increased nasal resonance.

Hyponasality. If your child has allergies, or enlarged tonsils and adenoids, she may breathe through her mouth. As a result, sounds may never be resonated through her nasal cavity. She will sound as if she has a perpetual "cold." This is known as hyponasal resonance or hyponasality. When the conditions causing the hyponasality are treated, the hyponasality should improve as well. An otolaryngologist (ENT) can diagnose and treat the medical conditions that may underlie resonance problems, such as swollen adenoids.

Hypernasality. Your child may resonate too many sounds through the nasal cavity if she has a short velum (soft palate area), flaccid or floppy muscles, or difficulty with velopharyngeal closure (the sealing off of the nasal cavity by the soft palate and throat wall muscles). This is known as hypernasality. With hypernasality, your child's speech would sound "twangy."

The speech-language pathologist can give your child muscle strengthening exercises to help her improve velopharyngeal closure. If the hypernasality is severe and affects intelligibility, it may be necessary to seek treatment from a maxillofacial or cleft palate team. These teams are usually made up of dental, medical, and speech specialists. They might prescribe a speech appliance, similar to a dental bridge, that would make velopharyngeal closure easier. Or they might recommend pharyngeal flap surgery, which also aids in the closure. Maxillofacial and cleft palate teams are usually located in university hospitals, children's hospitals, and dental schools. Your pediatrician should be able to refer you to one in your area.

The Effects of Surgery on Resonance. Any surgical procedure like a tonsillectomy or adenoidectomy that removes tissue in the oral-nasal-throat area can affect the resonance of speech. Consequently, any time otolaryngological surgery is being considered for your child, the possible impact on resonance should be considered carefully. If your child has normal resonance before surgery, it is possible that she will sound hypernasal following surgery and may require a period of speech therapy to train the muscles for velopharyngeal closure. If your child has hyponasality before surgery, the resonance will probably sound normal after surgery because air is now able to resonate through her nasal cavity for the /m/, /n/, and /ng/ sounds. But, if your child has hypernasality before surgery, it is possible that this hypernasality will increase following surgery. If your physician recommends tonsillectomy or adenoidectomy for your child, request that a speech pathologist be included on the team to determine whether follow-up therapy or other intervention will be needed. Although the need for surgery is a medical decision, the possible effects on speech should not be ignored.

Nonverbal Communication

Nonverbal communication plays an important role in how a message is understood. Eye contact, gestures, facial expressions, and other types of body language are all part of the message we transmit, and greatly aid understanding of speech by reinforcing the message. Vocal cues, such as verbal emphasis like "Let's go *now,*" or emotion in the voice also contribute to the message. If the speaker does not look at you, if her gestures do not go along with the message, if she stands too close or too far away, it will affect how you perceive the message. A detailed discussion of nonverbal communication is included in Chapter 7.

Pragmatics

Pragmatics—the social use of conversation and language—also affects the intelligibility of speech. Turn-taking, knowing how to make "repairs" when someone doesn't understand you, and staying on the topic are all pragmatic skills that influence whether your child's communication is understood. Good pragmatic skills can compensate somewhat for poor speech intelligibility; poor pragmatic skills can reduce speech intelligibility. Chapter 7 explores pragmatics in detail.

Increasing Speech Intelligibility

When your child is beginning to speak, it is important to encourage all of her attempts. The chapters on the one- to three-word language stages, therefore, suggest that you respond to the *meaning* of what your child is saying, and not correct her speech. When do you then begin to correct speech? Remember that from the start of your child's language learning, you have provided a correct model for your child. So, your child has been hearing your sounds produced correctly all along. Generally, the right time to begin correcting speech errors is when you know that your child can successfully correct the sound. If she knows how to say the sound correctly, it is fine to comment and correct her. If she would be unable to self-correct, it is not a good idea to correct her.

During any speech-motor practice activities, the movement *and* the sound can be corrected. For example, if you are looking in a mirror with your child and rounding your lips to say "oo," you can comment on your child's movement. ("Let's make our lips into a big round circle.") Another appropriate time to correct your child's speech production is when she can sometimes make a sound correctly, but at other times has difficulty. For instance, she can say "run" correctly but says "wabbit" for "rabbit." Make up a game in which you combine the words "run rabbit" and practice with her. You can also correct your child if she sometimes leaves out a sound in a word but at other times says it correctly. For example, she might say "po" sometimes and "pop" at other times. You can then remind your child to say the end sound in the word.

People with Down syndrome can continue to improve their intelligibility all their lives. Inclusion and the need to speak clearly to be understood by friends and later by co-workers is a major motivating factor for children and adults with Down syndrome (as well as their parents) to keep working on speech. You can help by not getting too accustomed to speech errors that you—but only you—can understand. That is, even if *you* understand her when she leaves out syllables, leaves off sounds, slurs sounds together, or talks too fast, it is still important to have her work on those words/sentences again so she doesn't get into careless habits. Other family members should also be instructed not to settle for less than your child's best speech production, to help her maintain her speech skills. It is a good idea to check periodically with teachers, acquaintances, and other people who don't know your child that well to see what they are able to understand and what aspects of her speech are difficult for them to understand.

While trying to improve your child's intelligibility, it is also important not to frustrate or humiliate her with corrections. Be discreet about correcting her in public if she might be sensitive to corrections. Don't make her keep repeating her order over and over for the waitress if you can understand her but she can't. In addition, her speech will often deteriorate when she is tired, or when she feels sick, and everyone has times when they feel tired or sick. As much as possible, work on speech in quiet, fun, and loving ways, so that your child will want to be understood and will work hard to always use her best speech.

As long as your child receives speech and language therapy, the speech pathologist can continue to work with her on intelligibility, as well as suggest home activities and recommendations about how and when to correct your child at home. Chapter 10 provides information about various therapeutic approaches the speech pathologist may use to improve intelligibility.

Augmentative Communication

Most children with Down syndrome eventually use speech as their primary method of communication. Often, however, a child's abilities to express herself verbally lag behind her abilities to understand others. In addition, a very few children with Down syndrome never are able to speak intelligibly. They may have severe mental retardation, severe hearing loss, or a severe motor programming (apraxia) or neuromuscular (dysarthria) problem which makes speaking very difficult or impossible. Whether speech intelligibility problems are temporary or lifelong, augmentative communication systems can give children invaluable help in getting their messages across.

Augmentative communication refers to all communication systems that supplement, assist, or replace speech. The most commonly used types of augmentative communication systems include:

- Gestural communication systems (sign language systems) that rely on symbolic or codified gestures;

- Language boards, which consist of pictures of different people, objects, or actions a child can point to in order to indicate her wants and needs;
- Computer systems, which use synthesized voices to "talk" for the child.

For children with Down syndrome, augmentative communication systems are most commonly used as temporary transitional systems during the early development of speech. Transitional augmentative systems are appropriate for children who are not beginning to use speech by twelve to eighteen months of age and who are becoming frustrated by their inability to be understood by parents, siblings, and others. This includes the majority of children with Down syndrome.

The augmentative communication system most often used as a transitional system with children with Down syndrome is Total Communication—the simultaneous use of sign and speech. Chapters 5 and 6 discuss how Total Communication can help children in the one-word to three-word stages express themselves. By the age of five, children with Down syndrome have usually outgrown the need to use signs as their primary communication system, but signs may continue to be helpful when a new language concept is introduced. For example, signs for prepositions are very visual and help children learn the concepts. Signs may also be useful as an adjunct to speech at times when it is hard for your child to get her message across verbally, such as when she is angry or tired, and may be used to cue words or actions. Signs may also be used when your child really wants to be understood clearly. But, signs are not usually the primary communication system for older children and adults with Down syndrome.

The other augmentative communication system that might be used to help your child make the transition to speech is the language or communication board. Communication boards are inexpensive, adaptable, and easy to change and update, as well as easy for the communication partner to decode. Communication boards may range from the simple to the complex, and the system may not even involve a "board." Some examples of communication boards are:

- photos of a container of orange juice, apple juice, and milk mounted on magnets on the refrigerator door so that your child can indicate her drink preference.
- line drawings of your child's favorite toys so that she can indicate her play preferences.
- small photos of relatives and line drawings of basic needs (bathroom, glass of water) inserted in the plastic pockets of a board book so that your child can call someone for help.
- symbols or alphabet letters painted onto a wooden board.
- commercial pictures of fast food items laminated and hung from a small key chain to enable an older child or adult to order food independently at her favorite fast food restaurant.

When a communication board is used as a transition to speech, it should be used following the Total Communication model. That is, use the board and the spoken word simultaneously with your child. When your child points to a picture, provide the verbal model: "You want to play your tape recorder now. I'll put the music on." A communication board might also be used as a supplement to speech. For instance, if your child's speech can be understood at home, but not by others, she might use a communication board at school, but use speech at home. If she frequently communicates with people in the community, such as day care workers or bus drivers who may not know sign language, or if she has difficulty with the motor skills needed to sign, communication boards offer another channel for communication.

The best communication boards are developed to meet the unique needs of a specific user. Pictures included on your child's board should be geared to her interests and vocabulary and should be updated frequently as her needs change. As a parent, you may develop a communication board for your child to use at home, or you may serve as a major source of information for the speech-language pathologist designing the communication board.

There are many materials available commercially that simplify the actual production of the communication board. These range from laminated folders to albums to plastic key chain tabs. There are photos, line drawings, and symbols that can be purchased in different sizes, shapes, and colors. The wide variety available makes it possible to meet the specific needs of any communication board user. You and the speech-language pathologist can work together to design the best system for your child. Sources for pictures and symbols that may be used on communication boards are provided in the resources section.

What if, for some reason, neither Total Communication nor a communication board works as a transitional communication system for your child? Or what if it appears that she may never be able to use speech intelligibly? In these cases, a computerized augmentation system may be recommended for your child. A wide range of computerized devices are available: some produce synthesized speech, while others produce a visual display on the computer screen; some are operated with a paddle or joystick, and others with a touch screen. Some of the most widely used communication systems are the *Handi-Voice*™, the *Touch Talker*™, the *WOLF*™, and the *Canon Communicator*™.

If a computer system is suggested for your child, you need advice from a professional with expertise in augmentative communication. Although most speech-language pathologists are knowledgeable in the use of Total Communication and language boards, they usually have not had extensive training in designing and prescribing computer systems. Also, the technology changes constantly. It is difficult, if not impossible, for someone who rarely prescribes augmentative communication systems to stay updated on all of the new devices.

Work with your speech-language pathologist. If she does not regularly prescribe augmentative systems, she can help you find a comprehensive augmentative communication center. These centers are located in various parts of the country. Staff members can provide a comprehensive augmentative communication evaluation to assess your child's needs and develop the best communication system to meet those needs. They will consult with and possibly even train your local professional, so that she will be able to follow through with your child for the long term. They will also train your family to use the communication system with your child. In addition, they can provide information about funding sources. Augmentative communication devices and services are now included under federal law. Some insurance companies or school systems will cover the cost of the evaluation, equipment, and training. Many local fraternal organizations such as the Lions Club, Knights of Columbus, or Sertoma will also help families purchase equipment.

There are national and international registries of professionals who specialize in the area of augmentative communication. There are organizations, meetings, technical fairs, newsletters, and even computer networks of augmentative communication "pen pals." Some important sources for information are provided in the Resources section.

Making Augmentative Communication Work

If your child uses an augmentative communication system, there are many ways you can help:

- Learn to use the augmentative system yourself.
- Use the system consistently with your child—always or at least as frequently as possible.
- If the system is being used as a transition to speech, always use speech simultaneously with the sign or picture board.
- Treat the augmentative system as a valid means of communication. Respond to the augmentative system as you would to speech.

- Reward your child's communication attempts. Repeat what she has said to validate, and within reason, respond to her requests.
- Be patient! Augmentative communication is slower than speech but your child's message will be worth waiting for.
- Encourage grandparents, day care workers, siblings, and others in your child's daily environment to learn the augmentative communication system and to respond to your child's communication attempts.

Facilitated Communication

Facilitated Communication is a relatively new communication system which was developed in Australia by Rosemary Crossley and brought to the United States by Dr. Douglas Biklen. Facilitated communication can use an alphabet board, a typewriter, or a computer keyboard to provide a communication system for people who have severe communication disabilities. An important part of the system is that the communicator works with a person who acts as the facilitator, who sits right next to, and usually slightly in back of, the child, and supports her hand, wrist, or elbow as she selects the letters to form the words. The facilitator might help to isolate the index finger for pointing, stabilize the elbow, or pull the arm back after the child has selected a letter. The facilitator appears to provide emotional as well as physiological support. The goal is to progress to the communication level of open-ended questions so that the facilitator may only have to ask, "Is there anything that you want to tell me about today?" Estimates are that it may take an hour or three months to develop fluency using this method.

Facilitated communication is currently used only for children or adults who cannot or do not communicate using other methods. The benefit of facilitated communication is that it enables people who were locked inside their own worlds to communicate. The system has been most widely used for children and adults with autism, but recently, facilitated communication has begun to be used with children and adults with Down syndrome who have not communicated through other means. Facilitated communication would generally not be used if the child is capable of using another communication system. It is a limiting system because the user cannot independently communicate, but needs to have the facilitator present, so it is difficult to use as a readily accessible daily communication system.

There are many unanswered questions and much controversy that surround the use of facilitated communication. What role does the facilitator play? Does it work? Who is really communicating? One of the criticisms of facilitated communication is that it relies on the questioning of the facilitator and, in many cases, also relies on the interpretation of the message by the facilitator. Often, the "speaker" produces some misspellings and equivocal statements, and the facilitator must interpret the results. Also, many children will only communicate with a specific facilitator, such as a parent or favored caretaker. We don't know where facilitated communication will lead in the understanding of language, thought, and intelligence, but it is certainly one of the most controversial and possibly promising communication techniques to surface in many years.

Technology has greatly expanded the opportunities for communication for all people. Every child with Down syndrome has something important to tell us. Fortunately, we are finally reaching the level of technology and understanding that will enable us to help each and every child communicate with the world.

Conclusion

Speech intelligibility is extremely important to your child's life because it affects her ability to be understood at home, in school, and in the community. There is a lot you can do to help your child improve her intelligibility. Your child will benefit greatly from your work with her on the motor, verbal, and nonverbal skills that affect whether her speech is understood. In addition, new technologies are making communication possible for children who cannot

develop intelligible speech. Today, there is really no child who cannot communicate with her world. If you understand speech intelligibility and the problems that can affect it, you will be prepared to help your child achieve the best possible speech intelligibility.

Resources on Intelligibility

Kumin, L. "Can You Say that Again? Issues in Intelligibility of Speech," paper presented at the National Down Syndrome Congress, September, 1991. (Tape can be ordered through NDSC).

Oetter, P. & Richter, E. (1988) MORE (whistles) Basic, Variety and Deluxe Kits - available from PDP Products, 12015 North July Ave., Hugo, MN 55038.

Swift, E. & Rosin, P. (1990) "A Remediation Sequence to Improve Speech Intelligibility for Students with Down Syndrome." *Language, Speech and Hearing Services in Schools*, *21*, 140-146.

Williams, C., Sbafchning, K., Polk, G. & Gleim, E. (1984) *99 Easy to Use Speech & Language Activities*. Tucson, AZ: Communication Skill Builders. Book has many activities and exercises for the articulators that can be used at home.

Organizations

Access Unlimited
3535 Briarpark Dr., Ste 102
Houston, TX 77042
Organization which provides resources for information on hardware and software for people with special needs.

Apple's Worldwide Disability Solutions Group
Apple Computer, Inc.
20525 Mariani Ave.
Cupertino, CA 95014
(800) 732-3131; (408) 974-7911
(408) 974-7911 (TDD)
In addition to information about Apple products, office maintains a data base of hardware, software, publications, and organizations.

Center for Special Education Technology
1920 Association Dr.
Reston, VA 22901
Publishes a monthly newsletter about technology and children with special needs.

Closing the Gap
P. O. Box 68
Henderson, MN 56004
612-248-3294
Resource center for technology information; publishes bi-monthly newsletter.

National Easter Seal Society
2023 West Ogden Ave.
Chicago, IL 60612
Organization which has a network of treatment centers throughout the United States; also publishes *Computer Disability News*.

National Support Center for Persons with Disabilities
IBM Corporation
P.O. Box 2150
Atlanta, GA 30055
(800) IBM-2133; (404) 988-2733 (TDD)

Resource center for information about IBM products for individuals with disabilities.

RESNA, The Association for the Advancement of
   Rehabilitation Technology
1101 Connecticut Ave., NW
Suite 700
Washington, D.C. 20036
(202) 857-1140
Information on Technology Assistance Projects in your state which can provide equipment, suggestions, and models of augmentative communication systems to help you and the SLP design a system for your child.

Technology for Language and Learning
P.O. Box 327
East Rockaway, NY 11518
Center promotes the use of computers for children with special needs; resources include a special education public domain software collection.

TASH, The Association for Persons with Severe Handicaps
11201 Greenwood Ave., North
Seattle, WA 98133
(206) 361-8870
Information and annual conference.

The U.S. Society for Augmentative and Alternative Communication
c/o Barkley Memorial Center
University of Nebraska
Lincoln, NE 68588
(402) 472-5463
Information and resources regarding augmentative communication, hardware, and software.

Waisman Center/Trace R & D Center
University of Wisconsin-Madison
1500 Highland Ave.
Madison, WI 53705-2280
(608) 262-6966
The Trace Resource Book provides information regarding nonvocal communication technological resources.

Sources for Symbols & Pictures for Communication Boards

Communication Sheets
American Guidance Service
Publishers Building
Circle Pines, MN 55014

Core Picture Vocabulary
Word Making Productions
70 West Louise Avenue
Salt Lake City, UT 85114

Food Photos
(people, actions, feelings, food)
Mayer-Johnson Co.
P.O. Box 1579
Solano Beach, CA 92075-1579

Help Me to Help Myself
Help Me to Help Myself Communication Aids
342 Acre Ave.
Brownsburg, IN 46112
(317) 852-4427

Peel and Put, Pictures Please Stickers
Imaginart Communication Products
P.O. Box 1868, 25680 Oakwood St.
Idyllwild, CA 92349
(714) 659-5905

Photo Sticks, Noun Sticks
(people, verbs, social interaction pictures)
Fred Sammons, Inc.
P.O. Box 32
Brookfield, IL 60513
(800) 323-7305

Pick 'N Stick Fast Food, Pocket Picture Holder, Touch 'N Talk Communication Board/Notebook, Pick 'N Stick Color Packs
(nouns, verbs, pronouns, modifiers)
Crestwood Company
331 South Third Street, Box 04513
Milwaukee, WI 53204

Picsyms
Don Johnson Developmental Equipment, Inc.
P.O. Box 639
1000 North Rand Rd., Bldg. 115
Wauconda, IL 60084-0639

Picture Communication Symbols
C.C. Publications, Inc.
Box 23699
Tigard, OR 97223-0108

Rebus Glossary (picture dictionary)
(furniture, food, toys, clothes, animals)
Communication Skill Builders, Inc.
313 North Dodge Blvd., Box 42050-H
Tucson, AZ 85733

Restaurant & Shopping Cards
Attainment Company
504 Commerce Parkway
Verona, WI 53593
(608) 845-7880

Talking Pictures, Passport to Independence
Baggeboda Press
107 North Pine Street
Little Rock, AR 72205

Word Making Stickers
Dairy Council of Metropolitan NY, Inc.
60 East 42nd Street
New York, NY 11165

Newsletters and Books About Electronic and Computerized Communication Devices

Beukelman, D. and Mirenda, P. (1992) *Augmentative and Alternative Communication: Management of Severe Communication Disorders in Children and Adults*. Baltimore: Brookes Publishing.

Burkhart, L. (1980) *Homemade Battery Powered Toys and Educational Devices for Severely Handicapped Children*. College Park, MD.

Burkhart, L. (1982) *More Homemade Battery Devices for Severely Handicapped Children with Suggested Activities*. College Park, MD.

Burkhart, L. (1988) *Using Computers and Speech Synthesizers to Facilitate Communicative Interaction with Young and/or Severely Handicapped Children*. College Park, MD.

Communication Outlook (Quarterly International Publication in Augmentative and Alternate Communication). Artificial Language Laboratory, Computer Science Department, Michigan State University, East Lansing, MI 48824.

9 | UNDERSTANDING SPEECH AND LANGUAGE EVALUATION

Introduction

In order to help your child with Down syndrome overcome or compensate for any language or speech problems he might have, he needs to be evaluated. Speech and language evaluations, or assessments, are the best way to identify the specific speech or language problems that may affect your child. That is why, for most parents and professionals, an assessment is the first step in treatment.

Speech and language evaluation is a process that can give you a realistic picture of your child's current speech and language skills and how he uses them. Different terms may be used to describe a speech and language evaluation such as assessment, diagnostic evaluation, and testing. The terms often cause anxiety for parents because testing involves scores, comparisons, and judgments about their child. It helps, however, to keep in mind that testing opens the door to treatment.

Assessment and treatment are best viewed as a continuous process. Assessment provides information for treatment and treatment results in changes in how your child communicates, which in turn affects his next assessment. It is useful to regularly update assessments so that the picture of your child's communication skills and your treatment plan stay current.

Why Assess?

Assessments may be performed for a variety of reasons and may occur at many different times throughout your child's life. Your infant or toddler's first evaluation may be through an agency such as Child Find or your local school district. The purpose of a Child Find evaluation is to document your infant's or child's speech and language skills in order to determine whether he is eligible for services according to the state guidelines. In Child Find (the name may vary from state to state—these are the programs that try to locate and identify children who need services) or other educational outreach programs, the diagnostic evaluation may be center-based or home-based. You may visit a diagnostic center or your local school, and the testing may be done during one or more sessions, or even during a period of diagnostic therapy lasting several weeks.

Your child's first diagnostic evaluation may be long and complex. It will determine your child's level of skill in various areas of speech and language prior to beginning therapy. It can then serve as a baseline to compare how much progress your child makes in the future. For example, initial testing may show that your child uses the /b/, /d/, /p/, /r/, and /m/ sounds. Future testing will document the new sounds your child adds to his repertoire.

An assessment may also be conducted to determine whether your child is eligible for services in a particular setting or from a particular agency. For example, an assessment through your local board of education (often referred to as the LEA, or "local education agency") is usually conducted for this purpose—to determine whether your child is eligible to receive services through the school system. Once enrolled, subsequent speech and language evaluations will probably be completed in your child's own school by his speech-language pathologist (SLP) as part of the annual educational review procedures. This is sometimes referred to as the IEP/ARD process. IEP refers to the Individualized Educational Program—your child's specific special education plan. ARD refers to the Assessment, Referral and Dismissal procedures—the procedures for placing children in special education. Usually, parents are not present for annual testing sessions, but are provided with the results at the IEP meeting held annually to review a child's progress and revise his educational plan.

There are other reasons for assessment. You may be curious to know whether a specific treatment program, such as myofunctional therapy, would benefit your child, and request an evaluation for that specific program. An assessment may also be conducted because you want a second opinion, you want what you consider to be a more independent evaluation, or you have been referred by your pediatrician for a speech and language evaluation. Most evaluations done through comprehensive centers for children with Down syndrome are based on physician referral, but you can request an assessment without a doctor's prescription.

Assessments may be ongoing and be conducted as part of your child's treatment plan. This type of assessment is sometimes referred to as "pre-testing" and "post-testing." Your child would first be tested on a specific skill, such as his ability to produce the "p" sound correctly. Then treatment would be given, followed by a post-test to determine whether he has mastered the "p" sound following treatment. This gives precise information about the effectiveness of a treatment approach or therapy.

General Guidelines—The Parent's Role

Because the purpose of the speech and language evaluation is to get an *accurate* picture of your child's communication skills, try to observe the evaluation session and be sure to tell the SLP if your child's performance is not typical of his usual communication. It may also be helpful to bring in audiotapes or videotapes of your child talking with family members at home, or to bring favorite toys or books to enable the SLP to observe your child in the most comfortable setting possible.Research has shown that children generally use longer phrases and sentences at home. So, if your observations of your child at home don't agree with the test results, talk with the speech-language pathologist.

Tests of communication depend on your child's cooperation and comfort level during the testing. An unfamiliar setting, fatigue, an ear infection, or a cold may alter your child's performance. It is very frustrating to observe an evaluation and know that your child is capable of understanding language, saying words, and completing a task, but is not performing at that level during test. Speak up! Any diligent professional is interested in getting accurate results, and you can greatly help by providing information. Where will the speech and language evaluation be conducted? How long will the testing last? Will it be done in one session or several? Ask lots of questions and offer lots about what you know about your child.

The process of diagnostic evaluations, especially the initial evaluation, may vary greatly depending on who is performing the evaluation and where it is performed. Frequently, in regional medical centers, the diagnostic evaluation will be completed in one to two days because your child is being evaluated by many specialists. During that period, he will be seen not only for speech and language evaluation, but also for evaluation by a pediatrician, psychologist, occupational therapist, physical therapist, and social worker. University-based settings will usually complete the evaluation in more than one session, and may even suggest a one-month period of diagnostic therapy for your infant or toddler to get a true picture of your child's typical speech and language skills over an extended time. Private practitioners and hospitals use many different models. School systems may use home-based or center-based (school or central office) evaluations. When the school system uses home-based evaluations, the SLP evaluates your child at home in his natural setting. The assessment may be completed in one or several sessions. The professional will bring the testing materials to your home, and will meet with you at home or in the center office for a follow-up session to share the results of the evaluation.

What Happens During Assessments?

Assessment begins the process of treating your child's speech and language problems. The assessment-treatment process usually begins with a diagnostic evaluation, and the first step in the evaluation process is the initial contact between the family and the school district or a Speech and Language Center or Department. After an

assessment request is received, the center will usually send a case history form or a pre-evaluation questionnaire to be returned prior to the diagnostic session. The center will usually also request that you send any relevant medical or developmental reports.

The Case History

Before a scheduled assessment, most SLPs, school districts, or centers will want to gather background information about your child. They will likely do this by a written questionnaire. The purpose of this form is to aid the SLP in preparing for the assessment. Questions usually address medical history, developmental history, social and family history, educational history, and behavioral history. They also ask for suggestions on how best to approach your child. For example, if your child is shy in new situations: will it help for your child to have a favorite stuffed animal with him; will it help to talk with him first to make him feel at ease; would it help to begin with a play activity? The case history form will also request information regarding his favorite books, toys, and foods. This form will be carefully read by the professional planning the evaluation;

so if you have any specific suggestions that will help in planning, be sure to include them when you return the form. Sometimes a comment, such as "My child loves Big Bird" or "My child will talk about Batman," will greatly assist the professionals whom your child is meeting for the first time.

Parent-Child Observation

When a parent and child arrive for the diagnostic evaluation, the first step is usually for the speech-language pathologist to observe them playing and talking together through a one-way mirror. In this setting, the child is usually most relaxed, and the professional is more likely to get an accurate view of his communication pattern. Many times, professionals have observed through the mirror an animated talkative child having fun with his mom, but when they come into the room and try to interact with him, they may get nowhere. Had they not observed the parent and child initially, they would have had an inaccurate impression of the child's communication skills.

During the observation, SLPs are particularly interested in observing the verbal and non-verbal interactions between you and your child, as well as turn-taking, questions and responses to questions, how your child gets attention, and how he gets his needs met through communication. Parents of young children need information on how to enhance communication; therefore it is essential for the SLP to know how parents interact with their child. The SLP needs to know how parents react to their child's communication. With older children, the observation enables the SLP to determine typical communication patterns. The observation would be videotaped and would be used to evaluate conversation skills, pragmatics, and non-verbal communication skills. The professional might look at the length of phrases and sentences, whether your child initiates conversation or only responds to your questions, and whether your child uses specific morphological endings. The observation, combined with information from a conversational sample (an actual transcript of your child's conversation), will also provide information on how intelligible his speech is, and whether his communication partners have difficulty understanding his speech.

Formal and Informal Assessment

Speech and language evaluations generally include both formal and informal assessments. In formal assessments, your child's performance on standardized tests is compared to the performance of other children; his performance is quantified and measured. During informal assessment, observation and conversational samples are used, among other techniques, to broaden the picture of your child's communication skills. Informal assessment attempts to describe rather than measure your child's communication skills and style.

The specific types of assessments used during informal and formal portions of the diagnostic evaluation will depend on your child's age and developmental level. For example, in young children, play with toys will be observed while in older children, toys or a book, or general conversation about a family trip or a favorite television show may be used to elicit a sample of conversation. For infants, the SLP would assess your child's language precursors, observe your child, and interview you. Speech tests, however, would not be appropriate. For a ten-year-old, speech tests that evaluate his ability to produce each speech sound and an assessment of voice and fluency would be appropriate.

The formal assessment is an important part of the diagnostic process. Because the instructions, test items, and scoring system are presented in exactly the same manner to each child tested, the formal assessment ensures that the information gathered about your child is reliable. Formal testing can provide information about the skills that your child has mastered, the skills that are emerging, and the skills for which your child will require treatment.

Standardized tests may be norm referenced or criterion referenced. Norm referenced tests compare your child's performance to the performance of between five hundred and fifteen hundred other children who were tested to establish the test norms. Comprehensive tests that sample a wide range of expressive and receptive language skills are usually norm referenced. One of the difficulties with norm referenced tests is that the norms are usually collected with typically developing children, not children with Down syndrome, so your child's scores can be compared only with those of typically developing children, not with scores from other children with Down syndrome. There is a need for developmental speech and language norms for children with Down syndrome, but, at present, they do not exist.

Tests that are criterion referenced measure how your child performs on a specific set of skills. A criterion referenced test might tell you which word endings your child has mastered and which word endings he has not yet mastered. Tests in speech and language for syntax, morphological skills, or auditory memory are typically criterion referenced. A criterion referenced test usually provides a list of the skills to be mastered in developmental order, so that the test can also be used over time to measure your child's progress in specific skill areas.

What is Assessed?

A comprehensive diagnostic evaluation should assess all speech and language skills appropriate to your child's age and developmental level. Most evaluations, however, will target only those skill areas being tested for. If the evaluation is for pre-or post-testing, it may sample only one skill, such as the ability to use plural word endings or the ability to produce the /g/ sound. Annual testing for the IEP/ARD process may target the speech and language goals from the last IEP to determine how much progress has been made. This section will address the areas of speech and language that are likely to be assessed at some point in your child's development. It will describe how each of the areas is generally evaluated, and provide insight into what the results mean. A separate section at the end of the chapter will discuss understanding assessment results.

Understanding Speech Evaluation

Because speech evaluations assess your child's verbal expression, you cannot evaluate speech until your child is actually speaking. There are, however, other developmental items to assess. Evaluations of infants and toddlers may include an assessment of the muscles for feeding or certain pre-speech skills, such as the ability to make a kissing sound, elevate the tongue, and close the mouth. The speech evaluation will also assess the structure and function of the muscles of the face, larynx, and pharynx.

Orofacial Structure and Function. The first section of the speech evaluation is the *Oral Peripheral Examination,* which usually includes assessment of the structure and function of the *orofacial muscles* (the muscles in and around the mouth and face), voice and resonance, and the respiratory support for speech. The purpose of this part of the evaluation is to determine whether there are any physical factors affecting your child's speech.

The SLP will observe your child's facial structure. She will comment on facial symmetry, on the appearance of the lips, and on the relative size and positioning of the maxilla (upper jaw) and mandible (lower jaw). She will examine the size of the tongue and its relative size compared to the mouth. She will examine the relationship of the upper and lower teeth, and any space (diastema) between the teeth. She will observe the length of the soft palate, and will look for any signs of cleft palate or sub-mucous cleft palate. She will then focus on how your child's lips and tongue work. To evaluate lips, your child will be asked to smile and to pucker up for a kiss. This allows the examiner to observe lip retraction and protrusion. To evaluate your child's control of the tongue muscles, your child will be asked to stretch his tongue toward his nose and toward his chin, put his tongue behind his teeth, touch the outside corners of his lips with his tongue, lick his lips as if licking off ice cream, and move his tongue toward a spot on each cheek after the examiner points to that spot. This allows the examiner to observe your child's tongue mobility and tongue control.

Voice and Respiration Evaluation. The SLP will ask your child to make the "ah" and "ee" sounds and hold them for as long as he can. The examiner is interested in listening to volume, clarity, voice quality, and the ability to sustain a vocal tone. She will also listen for hoarseness, breathiness, huskiness, pitch, and other vocal qualities. She may also use a Visipitch speech-viewer or other technology that displays vocal output on a screen. She will also assess the respiratory support for speech—that is, does the voice appear to be weak because there is insufficient breath? She will notice whether your child breathes from the abdomen, diaphragm, or thorax, or whether he elevates the shoulders in a shallow breathing pattern.

Resonance Function. The SLP will also evaluate your child's velopharyngeal closure ability (discussed in Chapter 8). She will try to determine whether sounds are produced through the nasal cavity or through the oral cavity. To evaluate resonance, the SLP may ask your child to say "ah" or "ee" and to hold the sound for as long as he can. The examiner will observe the movement inside the oral cavity and will evaluate the mobility of the velum (soft palate) and the effectiveness of the velopharyngeal closure. The examiner may hold a mirror under the nose or use the "see scape," a device that displays how air is emitted through the nasal cavity for nasal sounds. Follow-up assessment may include more formal resonance testing, using equipment such as a spirometer or a manometer to measure the effectiveness of the velopharyngeal closure.

Fluency Evaluation. The SLP will also be interested in evaluating the fluency of your child's speech. She may ask you or your child to fill out a questionnaire about situations in which fluency is a problem for your child. She may videotape or audiotape a conversation of your child reading a passage and then analyze his speech. She is seeking to determine whether your child has difficulty on certain sounds, in certain parts of sentences or conversations, or in certain situations. She will try to determine whether there is difficulty with the smoothness of the airflow, and whether there is muscle tension in various articulators. The evaluation will also assess your child's rate of speech. Is the rate slow, fast, or appropriate to the person and the situation?

If the speech evaluation does not find a fluency problem, but *you* hear a problem with stuttering, especially in conversations, make sure that you tell the SLP and if possible audiotape or videotape a situation where the fluency problem is likely to occur.

Articulation Evaluation. One of the major goals of the speech evaluation is to describe the sounds your child uses for speech and to identify any speech sound errors. Two general approaches are used. An articulation approach will use a test to systematically examine your child's production of each sound presented, usually in single words; for example, "*b*ox," "*b*aby," and "bi*b*." It may also include a conversational sample to evaluate how your child produces sounds in connected speech.

Articulation tests examine your child's production of each phoneme or sound of English, usually in single words. For example, pictures of the words, "*b*ox" and "ba*b*y" and "bi*b*" may be used to examine the child's production of the *b* sound when it is at the beginning, in the middle, or at the end of words. In professional lingo, this is referred to as the sound in the initial, medial, and final position. Based on the articulation test, you may be told that your child has difficulty with specific sounds and you will be told in which positions these errors occur. An example of a test result is:

C.P. has difficulty with the /s/ in the initial and final position, /l/ in the medial and final position, /r/ in the initial and final positions, and /g/ in the final position.

It is important to remember that most norms are developed based on single words. While typically developing children may have no more difficulty with a sound in a word when it is part of conversation, children with Down syndrome may be able to make sounds in single words, but may have much more difficulty in speech and conversation. For example, your child may say the word "cake" correctly when looking at a picture or reading the single word, but have difficulty with the word in "I want a chocolate birthday cake." It is also important to understand that the longer a child makes a sound incorrectly, the more strongly the incorrect movements and sounds are reinforced. If your seven-year-old child says /th/ for /s/, as in "thun" for "sun," for seven years, the /th/ sounds "right" to you and to him. His muscles are used to making the sound that way and it feels "right" to him to make that sound. So, even though the norms may report that the /s/ sound is acquired by typically developing children between ages seven and nine, it is preferable to work on producing that sound accurately as early as possible for children with Down syndrome in order to short-circuit possible problems.

In evaluating your child's speech, the SLP may use either the norms for children of your child's chronological age or the norms for children of his mental age. For example, if your child is seven but has a mental age of five, the SLP may compare his speech with the norms for a typically developing seven-year-old *or* a typically developing five-year-old. When mental age comparisons are made, children with Down syndrome often lose out on valuable speech-language services. This is because some early intervention and special education programs deny children speech therapy unless their speech skills are significantly below the norm. Clearly, if the norm used for your child is the norm for someone of his mental age, not chronological age, it will be harder for him to qualify. Your child's overall mental age is, after all, based on the age level at which he functions in many developmental areas, *including speech*. So, if your child has a mental age of five, he is likely to have speech skills at about the five-year level, and can therefore be denied speech therapy. But if the norm for someone of his chronological age of seven is used, he is much more likely to be found eligible.

Articulation and Distinctive Features Testing. There are tests used to describe problems with sounds. One method, known as the distinctive features approach, studies the features that sounds your child makes *incorrectly* have in common, by examining the place, manner, and voicing characteristics of the individual sounds. This testing looks at the pattern of errors that your child makes. For example, does your child have difficulty with all sounds that involve lifting the tongue tip, or all sounds that involve puckering and rounding the lips?

As Chapter 7 explains, all the sounds of English are produced:

- using specific articulators (place of production);
- emitting air in a certain way (manner of production); and
- either vibrating or not vibrating the vocal cords for the specific sound (voicing).

The distinctive feature system works especially well when describing the sound production of a child who has physical problems, such as muscle weakness, that affect articulation. If, for example, your child has difficulty with sounds that require closing the lips tightly and he cannot close his lips tightly, he will have difficulty with all sounds that involve closing his lips tightly. Looking at his production of each separate sound, therefore, cannot describe his problem as clearly as a distinctive feature analysis. Thus, when you are given the results, you will be told that your child has difficulty with plosive sounds, or with lingua-alveolar sounds (sounds made with the tongue tip on the gum ridge in back of the teeth). Treatment will then focus on the specific distinctive features that are difficult for your child. Distinctive features therapy is discussed in Chapter 10.

Stimulability Testing. Once the SLP has catalogued your child's articulation sound by sound, stimulability testing will be performed. This is a brief examination of whether your child can imitate a sound correctly even though he cannot yet produce the sound correctly in his own speech; for example, he can say /s/ in imitation, but does not use the sound in his own speech. Stimulability testing provides the SLP with information about which sounds are emerging in your child's speech and which sounds may be easy to teach in therapy. Some therapists wear a clown's hat and tell your child that they are going to make some funny sounds; then they produce the sound and ask your child to repeat it. Others simply ask your child to repeat the sounds after them. Usually, only sounds your child was *not* able to produce on the articulation test are tested for stimulability, but some professionals test all consonant and vowel sounds for stimulability. The results will usually be reported to you in the following form:

> "Your child is stimulable on three of his error sounds"; or

> "He is stimulable on the /p/,/k/, and /f/ sounds, but not on the /s/ and /r/ sounds."

When your child is able to imitate a sound, you may be able to stimulate that sound at home, using some of the suggestions provided in Chapter 7.

Diadochokinesis Testing. Diadochokinesis means the ability to make rapid alternating movements of the articulators, such as those need for longer words and phrases. For example, words like "cheeseburger" and "french fries" require diadochokinetic ability. These skills are based on muscle strength, accuracy, and coordination. As part of the evaluation, the SLP will look at your child's ability to make the rapid movements needed for speech, such as elevating his tongue as in the word "top." This is often a complex task for children with Down syndrome because they have difficulty in coordinating the rapid movement of the articulators. This is one of the reasons your child may be able to pronounce a sound in a single word, but have difficulty when it appears in a conversation. Usually, this skill will be tested by asking your child to repeat the following syllables as fast as he can until the SLP says stop:

- *puh* as in putt;
- *tuh* as in tuck; and
- *kuh* as in cup.

The SLP will count the number of times your child is able to produce each syllable in a five-second period. Your child will then be asked to repeat what the SLP says; she will then combine the syllables—puhtuhkuh, and ask him to say this "silly word" as quickly as he can for five seconds. If your child has difficulty with puhtuhkuh, she may instead ask him to say the word *buttercup* as quickly as he can. These syllables test the ability to rapidly move the articulators for front, middle, and back sounds. You will be told that your child is able to or has difficulty with making rapid alternating movements. Oro-motor and myofunctional therapy, discussed in Chapter 10, address problems in this skill area.

Intelligibility Testing. Intelligibility testing involves evaluating how easy or difficult it is for an unfamiliar listener to understand your child's speech. Intelligibility scores may be recorded as percentages (for example, "fifty percent intelligible") or as good, fair, or poor (for example, "fair intelligibility"). Sometimes, a formal assessment of intelligibility such as *The Weiss Comprehensive Intelligibility Test* may be used. Usually, a taped conversation sample is used to evaluate intelligibility. Intelligibility testing is really not "testing" at all, but rather a different way of analyzing your child's speech.

Phonological Process Analysis. Another approach to evaluating the sound-making abilities of your child is through phonological process analysis. This is a method of analyzing sound errors in speech by exploring the sound simplification rules or the substitution patterns your child uses. A phonological process analysis might look at, for example, whether your child makes all sounds in the front of the mouth, reduces all consonant blends to single sounds (pronouncing "sprinkle" as "finkle"), or whether he leaves off all of the final sounds in words. Suppose that your child can produce the /p/ sound and the /t/ sound, but he says /ca/ for "cat," and /ca/ for "cap." What if he also says /sto/ for "stop" and /po/ for "pot." The problem here is *not* that he is incapable of producing a correct /p/ or /t/ sound. He says the /p/ sound correctly in "pot" and says the /t/ sound correctly in "stop." The problem is that he leaves out the sound whenever it is at the end of words. These types of errors are described as phonological process errors. There are two types of tests that are commonly used to evaluate phonological processes: direct testing using objects and pictures and testing that evaluates your child's conversation.

Language Assessment

Language assessment is usually accomplished through both formal and informal testing. Formal language testing may involve a comprehensive battery such as the *Sequenced Inventory of Communication Development* or *Test of Language Development*. In addition, there are tests for a specific language skills, such as auditory processing of commands and the use of morphological word endings, such as plurals and past tense.

Informal assessment allows the SLP to get another view of your child's communication ability. This portion of the evaluation is usually audiotaped or videotaped so that it can be analyzed. With an infant, toddler, or younger child, toys will be used and activities that are above, below, or at age level will be presented to analyze the language skills your child has mastered or that are emerging. With older children, the informal assessment would include a conversational sample. The SLP and your child might discuss a favorite activity, or a favorite television program, movie, or vacation trip. It is important for you to provide information to the SLP regarding topics of interest to your child.

The informal language evaluation will include the following testing areas:

- Level of Play (younger child);
- Level of Attention;
- Receptive Language Skills;
- Expressive Language Skills;
- Pragmatic Skills; and
- Analysis of Conversation (older child)

Level of Play. Why do SLPs evaluate your child's play skills during a language evaluation? Evaluation of play tells therapists a lot about your child's cognitive level and his readiness for certain language tasks. It also provides information crucial to planning therapy activities that are at the appropriate play level for your child. For example, in working on turn-taking, would rolling a ball back and forth be more effective than pretend play with a toy farm.

Play is usually evaluated by using an observation scale that lists different levels of play, from exploratory play in which infants use their senses to explore an object by looking, touching, and mouthing, through the level of pretend play with objects, and up to the level of complex games with rules and socio-dramatic play. During the evaluation, the examiner will engage your child in play.

Level of Attention. This evaluation determines how long and how intensely your child focuses on toys or objects he is playing with. The purpose of evaluating your child's level of attention is to determine how best to present stimuli during therapy in order to maximize your child's learning. For example, will having all of the items for a therapy session in the room distract your child? Should there be only one toy in the room at a time? Can stations be set up around the room with your child and therapist moving from activity to activity? Can your child focus on a toy, object, or activity for seconds or minutes? What does he do to indicate that he is finished with the object and wants to move on to another activity? For older children, what is the length of a story that can be used in therapy? How long can a child focus on an activity or a conversation?

Receptive Language Skills. Receptive language tests measure what your child can understand. This includes both receiving and interpreting messages. In addition, through observing your child's play and his ability to follow instructions, an informal evaluation can be made of his receptive language ability. Informal assessment will ask questions like whether he follows one-stage commands but not two-stage commands and whether he understands "wh" questions. Receptive language tests range from single-word vocabulary tests to tests in which your child's ability to follow complex directions is assessed. Examples of tests commonly used for children with Down syndrome in the area of single-word vocabulary tests are the *Peabody Picture Vocabulary Tests (PPVT)* and the *Receptive One-Word Picture Vocabulary Test*. Other tests target specific receptive language skills such as the ability to follow instructions. *The Boehm Test* and *the Token Test for Children* are examples of this type of test.

Expressive Language Skills. Assessment of expressive language skills examines everything your child does to communicate. For example, an informal language evaluation of an infant would examine how your child points to a bottle to indicate that he wants it, or how he lifts up his hands to indicate that he wants to be taken out of his crib. These both are expressive skills. With older children, their use of Total Communication would be considered including any signs or gestures they use to communicate. With school-age children, appropriateness of vocabulary and level of syntax and morphology would be assessed using line drawings, and by taking conversational samples.

Tests of expressive language will assess your child's speech and language output. They may range from tests of single-word vocabulary such as the *Expressive One Word Picture Vocabulary Test* to tests (e.g., *CELF*) of complex language such as the ability to explain idioms or proverbs. Criterion referenced tests may evaluate your child's expressive output in a specific area of language such as syntax.

Another measure often used is MLU, or "mean length of utterance." MLU represents the average number of morphemes your child uses in his speech. For example, the SLP may report that

your child has a MLU of 2.0. This means that the average length of your child's phrases and sentences is 2.0 morphemes, as in "get coat," "go now," "want cheese," "railroad," and "birthday."

Receptive-Expressive Gap. Assessment may uncover that your child has a receptive-expressive gap. This means that he understands more language than he expresses. This is one of the most important findings that an assessment can yield. This information may be very helpful in documenting your child's need for services in the area of expressive language. Make sure your child's assessment results provide this information.

Pragmatic Skills. Informal language assessments evaluate pragmatics in younger children by observing what they do to get their message across, including using pantomime or pointing. In addition, pragmatic evaluations will examine the use of pre-linguistic skills such as turn-taking. In older children, the pragmatics evaluation would look at primarily conversational skills by evaluating a videotaped conversation for turn-taking, topic maintenance, topic introduction, and awareness of listener needs for information. It would also include an analysis of nonverbal communication skills such as eye contact. Pragmatics are usually evaluated using observations and checklists.

Understanding Assessment Results

Once the speech and language evaluation has been completed, the SLP may discuss the results of the evaluation with you in person or may send a written report. It is best if both are used, so that you not only can review the report, but also can ask questions, ask for further information, and provide input about your home observations that may add important information to the evaluation. For example it is never too late in the evaluation to tell the SLP that your child's voice is hoarse at the end of the day, or that he stutters in new situations. It is also important to provide information about speech and language skills that your child uses at home but did not demonstrate during the evaluation. The meeting may be held at the end of the assessment, but will more likely be held at least a week after the evaluation. During the meeting, you will discuss the results of the diagnostic evaluation. The parent-child observation will be discussed, formal speech and language test results will be provided and explained, and the informal language assessment will be summarized.

The results of articulation testing, the oral peripheral, stimulability, and diadochokinesis and intelligibility measures will be discussed. When articulation results are reported to you, they may be presented as a sound-by-sound analysis ("your child had difficulty with /s/ in the initial and final positions"), a distinctive feature analysis ("your child had difficulty with sounds involving tongue tip elevation"), or a phonological processes analysis ("your child had difficulty with final consonant deletion").

Developmental data may also be provided based on test results. When you are given the results, you may be told "Your child has difficulty with the /s/ sound in initial and final position, but you don't need to worry because that sound is typically not developed until age eight." In my opinion, this does not mean that you should forget about therapy for /s/ until age eight because developmental articulation data may be misleading when applied to articulation in children with Down syndrome.

Developmental articulation norms may not be appropriate when assessing children with Down syndrome. First, there is no one standard set of articulation norms. That is, there is not total agreement about the ages at which specific sounds such as /f/, /s/, or /r/ are learned. So, it is possible that one SLP will say that your child's sounds are age appropriate while another will say that your child's sound production is delayed. Another problem with using developmental articulation norms is that the norms were set based on a sample of typically developing children, not on a sample of children with Down syndrome. Consequently, factors like low muscle tone and hearing were not considered when setting the norms. Further, some norms consider a sound to be "acquired" if a child can produce it 75 percent of the time, while other norms require 90 percent. Because of this confusing use of norms, when assessment results are expressed developmentally, ask questions to ensure that you understand exactly what the results mean for *your* child's speech production. Ask whether your child's performance is being compared to norms for chronological or for mental age. Ask for a copy of the norms and be sure that the same norms are used for subsequent testing. Ask whether your child's speech production was evaluated for muscle weakness and sequencing difficulties, in addition to age comparisons. Never rely just on developmental norms.

Understanding Test Scores

As a parent, you have specific needs for information. You will doubtlessly have questions you want answered. "What do these test results mean? What information can the results provide about my child's speech and language skills? For what purposes will the test results be used? What services will be provided based on these results?" You, your child's SLP, and your local school district will want to use the results to plan a specific speech and language intervention program. Be sure you understand clearly what the test scores and the results mean, and do not be shy about asking enough questions for you to understand the information. When you are given the test results, scores may be reported as developmental age scores, developmental quotients, percentile rankings, or standard scores, depending on how the specific test is scored and how the results are calculated. Ask questions like "What does a specific score mean? Does an Expressive Language Quotient Score of four years mean that my child performed at the level of a four-year-old? Does a sixtieth percentile score mean that he answered 60 percent of the questions correctly, 60 percent incorrectly, or that he performed better than 60 percent of the children on whom the test results were based?"

What Next? Results, Referrals, and Service

The purpose of speech and language evaluations varies in different situations. If the assessment is to determine whether speech and language services are needed, the evaluation should provide information that can be used directly to design an appropriate treatment plan. Testing can pinpoint areas in which your child needs help, and areas of strength that can be used to help your child develop good speech and language skills. If the assessment was done to evaluate your child's progress in a therapy program, the therapy program will already be in place and the assessment will provide information on how to modify that therapy program. The assessment may also point out the need for referrals to other specialists, such as a developmental pediatrician, otolaryngologist (ear, nose, and throat specialist), audiologist, neurologist, pedodontist (children's dentist), or orthodontist.

If it is determined that your child does not qualify for services, the speech language pathologist may suggest re-evaluating your child in six months or one year to check on your child's communication skills. Eligibility for free public services through your local school district depends on the evaluation. Your child may not be "eligible" for services, but may still "need" services. These tricky eligibility and need issues are discussed in Chapter 10.

Assessment can be very confusing, and can be emotionally exhausting for both you and your child. However, if you remember two facts, things will go better. First, always remember that you know your child best; you have much to contribute to a realistic understanding of your child's speech and language skills and needs. Second, always remember (and make sure the testers remember, too) that the goal of assessment is not endless data collection, but rather useful, practical information and insight into your child. You need information that you and the professionals can put to use to help your child's speech and language skills grow. Good evaluations provide this. Settle for nothing less.

10 | UNDERSTANDING SPEECH AND LANGUAGE TREATMENT

Speech and language therapy is essential for most children with Down syndrome to maximize their communication potential. Dr. Allen Crocker of Children's Hospital of Boston, a leading expert on people with Down syndrome, has stated that socially appropriate behavior *and* the ability to communicate and be understood are the two most important factors affecting the quality of life for a person with Down syndrome. Speech and language services should be provided routinely for infants, toddlers, young children, children, adolescents, and adults with Down syndrome. At some points in development, working on language development and language skills will take priority; at other stages, speech skills will take priority. In the early years, intense services facilitate language development. At later ages, children and adults should be monitored regularly by a professional who can provide help as needed, especially in the areas of speech intelligibility and pragmatics, throughout life.

Your role in speech and language development is critical. The professional who can provide information, assessment, and intervention to assist you is the certified speech-language pathologist (SLP). Ideally, you and a SLP will work together as partners to address the speech and language needs of your child with Down syndrome. However, not everyone has access to programs that involve parents in treatment. The speech and language services provided to your child may involve the SLP consulting with the classroom teacher, individual or group sessions, or demonstrations, information sessions, and training for you. As a parent, you need to be informed, and good ways to do this include reading books, attending workshops, and talking to other parents and professionals.

The Speech-Language Pathologist

Whether your child receives speech and language services through your local school, private practice, or another setting, you want to ensure that a qualified professional works with your child. To qualify for professional credentials (Certificate of Clinical Competence in Speech-Language Pathology, CCC-SLP), awarded by the American Speech-Language-Hearing Association, SLPs must complete an undergraduate and graduate level program that includes intensive supervised clinical practice with children and adults in the areas of speech, language, and hearing assessment, and remediation. They must pass a national certification examination, and complete a clinical fellowship training year (CFY) following graduation. If the professional lists "CCC-SLP" following her name, you know that she has completed a rigorous professional program.

You and the SLP will need to work very closely to help your child achieve maximum success in communication, so it is essential that you have a comfortable and trusting relationship. There needs to be a feeling of sharing and teamwork. The lines of communication need to be open and used on a regular basis. It is important to be able to ask questions and feel that the SLP is well trained to answer those questions.

You need to be directly involved in developing communication goals with the SLP so that the skills taught will be useful in your child's daily life. You also play a key role in helping your child achieve the goals. Your child may receive services through the school system, private practitioners, university centers, or rehabilitation centers, or a combination of settings, such as speech and language therapy in school and sessions provided by private SLPs. If you observe your child's therapy regularly, or are present in the therapy room, you and the SLP will probably communicate regularly. If you bring your child to a private practitioner or a rehabilitation center, ask that the SLP leave some time after each session to talk with you. You need to be updated after each session to stay abreast of the goals, your child's progress, and the activities of each session, as well as what home activities you might try that week. Even if the SLP shortens the therapy session to talk with you, it is worth the time; you will be able to follow through on the therapy goals for that week and will gain knowledge that can help your child.

If your child is receiving therapy through school, you will probably not observe her therapy sessions on a regular basis. How can you, then, maintain open lines of communication? Discuss with the SLP, from the very beginning, what would be the best way to communicate. Some parents and therapists send a notebook, log, or journal back and forth from each session. This provides information to parents and enables them to provide feedback and suggestions to the SLP. Other parents and professionals prefer to communicate by phone, weekly or monthly progress reports, or periodic meetings.

The most important factors in communication between parents and SLPs are honesty, a willingness to share information, and frequent contact. It is important for you to maintain frequent communication with your child's SLP; if meetings are infrequent, they are likely to be more formal and less open. Infrequent communication usually focuses on problems, not triumphs. A common concern of parents is that, with only annual meetings to evaluate the IEP, these meetings tend to focus on problem areas and how therapy will remedy the problems. More frequent meetings are more balanced between successes and difficulties, and may even help prevent problems.

Understanding Speech and Language Treatment and Prevention

Infants and children with Down syndrome receive speech and language therapy primarily for two reasons: 1) to prevent speech and language problems and 2) to remedy speech and language problems. These reasons apply regardless of your child's age.

Early speech and language intervention for infants and toddlers is usually intended as prevention. Young children with Down syndrome may be seen because they are considered to be "at risk" of developing speech and language delays. Early language stimulation and techniques such as Total Communication may prevent some communication problems. For example, in speech therapy, the prevention approach would teach your child to round her lips on the "oo" vowel sound even before she shows difficulty producing that sound. In language therapy, the prevention approach would teach your child greetings when they are appropriate for her to use, but before they have become a problem.

With older children, an approach called "remediation" is generally used. Speech and language problems are documented; then therapy is designed to "remedy" those problems. For example if your child substitutes /d/ for /g/ (as in the words "do," and "go"), speech therapy works on teaching the /g/ sound. In language therapy, the remediation approach would teach your child the proper pronoun form and the correct verb ending for the word "runs" if she says "him run" instead of "he runs." Although speech and language therapy are discussed separately in this chapter, they are usually provided at the same time as part of the same session. The balance between speech and language therapy will depend on your child's individual needs, skills, and age.

Understanding Speech Treatment

Regardless of where speech therapy is provided or by whom, you need to understand what actually happens during a therapy session. The first thing to understand is that what happens during

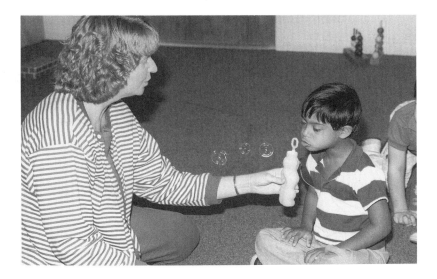

speech therapy depends entirely on what speech problems or skills are being worked on at the time. Many different speech problems and skills can be worked on, and many different approaches to therapy can be used with children with Down syndrome. This section reviews the different methods of speech therapy most often used for children with Down syndrome.

Treatment for speech may address the areas of articulation, oromotor skills (the term for problems related to low muscle tone and motor programming discussed in Chapter 8), voice, resonance, or fluency. Speech therapy may be provided individually or in small groups, within the classroom as part of the school program, or, as discussed above, by professionals in different centers. The types of speech therapy include: 1)articulation therapy 2)voice and resonance therapy, 3)fluency therapy, and 4)rate therapy. The following sections explain these different therapy types.

Articulation Therapy

The goal of articulation therapy is to remedy problems your child has producing specific sounds. The therapy approaches typically used to improve articulation include traditional articulation approach, distinctive features approach, phonological processes approach, and coarticulation approach.

Traditional Articulation Therapy. Traditional articulation treatment focuses on one or more sounds your child does not produce accurately and works on each in the different positions (beginning, middle, end) it appears in words. Examples of some goals of articulation therapy using the traditional approach are:

- Your child will be able to identify the /f/ sound when it is heard in the initial position in words 90 percent of the time (*f*un, *f*ive);
- Your child will be able to produce the /s/ sound in the initial position in words 90 percent of the time (*s*un, *s*ix);
- Your child will be able to produce the /k/ sound in the final position in words 90 percent of the time (bi*k*e, li*ck*); and
- Your child will be able to carry-over correct production of the /t/ sound in initial and final positions in words to conversation.

In the traditional approach, your child's errors will be identified according to the sound in error, such as /s/, the type of error production, such as "omission," and where in words the error occurs, such as the final position. Examples of descriptions of error sounds are:

- Your child substitutes /th/ for /s/ in the initial and final positions in words (he says *th*un for sun and i*th* for ice);
- Your child substitutes the /f/ for /th/ in the medial and final positions in words (he says too*f* and too*f*brush for tooth and toothbrush);
- Your child omits the /l/ in the initial position in words (he says ight for light); and
- Your child distorts the /s/ sound in all positions in words (he produces the s sound incorrectly in *s*un, ba*s*eball, and i*ce*).

With the traditional approach, your child will first be taught to listen for and identify the correct sound production when she hears it, then she will be taught to produce the sound through phonetic placement. In phonetic placement, your child is taught *how* to produce the sound correctly in isolation, such as /p/. Then she is taught to produce the sound in nonsense syllables in a specific position, such as "poo"; then in a specific position in words, such as "pie"; and then in the same position in phrases, such as "lemon pie"; and then in the same position in sentences, such as "I want lemon pie please"; and then finally in conversation. This process is followed for each sound in error in each position in which it occurs; this makes the traditional approach slow and tedious.

Another method which is widely used is the auditory discrimination method. This therapy concentrates on helping your child hear the difference between correct and incorrect sound productions; for example, the difference between "too*f*" and "tooth"). As mentioned above, with children with Down syndrome, the problem is usually *not* that they cannot hear the difference between two sounds. Instead, the problem may be that they do not know *when* to make a particular sound. Traditional articulation therapy and auditory discrimination are slow and tedious and do not remedy the underlying movement or perception problem; they merely address the symptoms of the problem. In my professional experience, I have found that traditional articulation treatment or the exclusive use of auditory discrimination do *not* work well for children with Down syndrome.

Distinctive Feature Approach. With the distinctive feature approach, the sounds your child uses are analyzed in a different way. Distinctive feature analysis categorizes the type of errors in sound production according to whether they are errors in the place of production, the manner of production, or voicing (discussed in Chapter 8). For example, does your child have difficulty raising her tongue tip to produce sounds such as /t/, /d/, /n/, and /l/, or making a plosive sound such as /p/, /b/, /k/, and /g/, or making a voiced sound such as /d/, /v/, and /z/? Therapy then focuses on teaching your child that specific skill, such as raising the tongue tip. The basis of distinctive features therapy is the generalization hypothesis. According to this theory, if your child masters the skills needed to make a sound in a specific place, manner, or voicing pattern, she will be able to use the same place, manner, or voicing in making other sounds. She will be able to generalize the skill that she has learned. Let's say, for example, that your child learns in therapy to raise her tongue tip and to correctly make the /t/ sound. If she generalizes, she will be able to elevate the tongue tip when she produces other sounds that involve the tongue tip, such as /d/, /l/, and /n/.

The distinctive features approach is a very logical, organized way of teaching sounds when the errors are based on neuromuscular problems such as low muscle tone. It makes sense that if your child cannot raise the tongue tip for /t/, she probably won't be able to raise the tongue tip for /l/. Targeting a feature in therapy is also usually a more rapid method for achieving results than a sound by sound approach.

Phonological Process Approach. Your child may be able to produce a sound correctly in isolation, or when the sound appears in certain words or in certain parts of words but not in others. For example, if your child says /ba/ for bat and /ba/ for ball, but can say "take" and "lake," she may not need to work on the /t/ and the /l/ sound in the final position in words. Instead, she may need to work on including the final sounds in words so that, for example, she says "ball" instead of /ba/. Testing can determine whether your child has difficulty producing these sounds, or whether the difficulty occurs because those sounds are in the final position in words.

Identifying the phonological process patterns used by children with Down syndrome is important because there are therapy methods that can help with the problems. Therapy for phonological processes is a cognitive type of therapy which works on increasing your child's awareness and use of sounds that she can make in some contexts but not in others. Through games and activities, therapy teaches your child when to make a selected phonological process, such as producing a final sound in a specific word. Chapter 8 discusses phonological processes in more detail and includes descriptions of activities you might do both in therapy and at home.

Coarticulation. In this therapy approach, the SLP looks not only at the sounds your child has trouble with, but also at the contexts in which the errors occur *and* the contexts in which your child can make the sound easily. For example, it is often easier for a child to produce an /s/ sound when it is followed by a /t/ sound, such as "*st*oop" rather than "*s*oup." Instead of teaching your child how to produce a sound, coarticulation therapy tries to find a context in which your child is already producing the sound correctly. Then, through therapy your child learns to transfer that correct sound production to other word contexts in which she was not making the sound correctly. For example, if your child can say "stop," the SLP will work with her on combining that word with other "s" contexts she cannot say, such as "stop soon," "stop soap," "stop bus."

Voice and Resonance Therapy

Voice and resonance therapy is used to correct voice and resonance problems identified during your child's assessment. The most common voice problems, laryngeal conditions or damage from vocal abuse such as shouting, are treated by the SLP along with the pediatrician, otolaryngologist, and maxillofacial specialists. Medical treatment may include surgery, medication, or a speech appliance. The most common resonance problems include hyponasality and hypernasality. See Chapter 8 for an explanation of these problems.

Therapy for voice and resonance problems includes orofacial, laryngeal, or pharyngeal exercises to strengthen the muscles used for voice and resonance. Specific exercises may focus on strengthening the palate muscles in order to decrease hypernasality or strengthening the adductor muscles of the larynx in order to reduce breathiness. Equipment such as the "Visipitch™"

or the "IBM Speech Viewer™" may be used to give your child feedback as she does the exercises.

Fluency Therapy

Your child may need fluency therapy if she "stutters"—if she repeats sounds, words, or portions of words, or has periods of silence during which she seems to be struggling to produce a sound. Fluency therapy will be designed specifically for the particular fluency problems that your child demonstrates. The cognitive approach to therapy, which analyzes the situations and stressors that lead to dysfluency, is less successful with children with Down syndrome because their dysfluency may not be common to specific situations. For example, dysfluencies may *not* occur only in school or only when your child talks on the telephone. A method that is effective in teaching smooth breathing and speech patterns, called "gentle onset" (this method may also be called "gentle attack" or "relaxed production"), has been more successful with the dysfluencies of children with Down syndrome. This is because dysfluency in children with Down syndrome appears to be related to muscle coordination and other neurophysiological factors, not to stress. Gentle onset works to relax the muscles used for voice, respiration, and articulation.

Rate Therapy

Rapid rate of speech is common in children with Down syndrome and it contributes to difficulty with intelligibility. The SLP may work on rate using demonstrations and material such as drums, a metronome, table-tapping, or rhythm added to speech. She may also use a musical melody to accompany speech (melodic intonation therapy), a pacing board, or a model that shows your child her rate of speech, such as a slow and fast moving toy truck. All of these methods are described in detail in the Home Activities section of the Chapter 8. Once your child is taught the concept of slow and fast speech and uses a slower rate, practice in using the new slower speech pattern will help to incorporate the slower rate into everyday speech.

Understanding Language Treatment

Children with Down syndrome receive language therapy for the same type of reasons they receive speech therapy: to help them learn language skills and to solve problems with language development. Virtually any age person—from birth through adolescence and beyond—can benefit from language therapy.

Because language is so critical to the future success of your child, it is important to monitor her language development closely. In the early years, therapy may focus on prelinguistic skills. Chapters 3 and 4 discuss language therapy and home activities for the precursors to spoken language. Therapy during the birth to three-word period usually focuses on training you to facilitate your child's language development and on changing your child's environment so that there are a lot of opportunities for learning and using language skills. Early language therapy usually uses Total Communication to help your child make the transition to speech while providing a viable communication method to express her new language skills.

Language therapy for children beyond the three-word stage is generally aimed at remedying specific language problems that have been identified during an assessment. Often therapy is designed just to solve one "problem" at a time. For some children with Down syndrome, this approach is adequate. For most, however, it is preferable to determine what language skills your child needs now and what language skills she will need to be successful as an adolescent and adult, and then to work on those skills.

The SLP will provide language therapy. The areas of language development that will be addressed—depending on your child's needs—include phonology, morphology, syntax, semantics, pragmatics, and non-verbal communication. Phonology is discussed in Chapter 9.

Morphology

Morphemes are most often worked on in therapy through the use of "pattern practice" or repetitive practice exercises. For example, if your child is working on "ing," she will name groups of pictures of people jump*ing,* runn*ing,* or walk*ing.* Or two therapists might work together and model the responses for your child. "What is Anna doing? She is jump*ing.*" In group therapy, children might take turns running, jumping, or walking, while the other children describe what they are doing. "Cory is jump*ing,* Becky is hopp*ing,* or Elizabeth walk*ing.*" Morpheme practice lends itself to home practice, so be sure to ask which morphemes are currently being targeted in therapy.

Syntax

Syntax is frequently worked on in therapy through pattern practice and through play activities using manipulative toys such as a play farm or schoolhouse. For example, toy "people" may be moved around to practice the concepts of "in front of" and "in back of." The SLP may ask, "Where is Grover?—In front of the line." "Where is Grover now?—In back of the line." For older children, action figures can be used in the same way, or dolls, stuffed animals, or trucks. Syntax is also worked on in therapy through the use of published programs such as *Syntax One* or the *Fokes Sentence Builder,* which provide structured practice materials. The *Fokes Sentence Builder* kit contains index cards with pictures and words which are organized in a series of file boxes. For example, there is a "who" box, an "is doing" box, and a "what for" or "to whom" box. When a card is taken from each box, the pictures and words provide cues to help your child practice correctly structured sentences, such as *"The girl / is throwing / the ball / to the dog."* The kit can also be used to practice a single structure, such as indirect objects, by keeping all the pictures constant except those from the "to whom" box. For example, your child could practice, "The girl is throwing the ball *to the dog* or *to the boy* or *to the man* or *to the clown* or *to the grandmother.*"

Semantics

Therapists usually work on semantics through goal-oriented activities, language experience activities, or in conjunction with classroom teachers on activities related to school subjects. Goal-oriented activities are therapeutic activities designed to help your child's language skills in several areas, including semantics. These activities have a beginning and an end. For example, making a Valentine's Day card or dressing a toy doll are good bases for language activities. Vocabulary, syntax, and other goals can be made part of the session. For example, how do you ask for crayons for the Valentine's Day card, what colors do you need, and which prepositions are useful to describe dressing the doll? The SLP will work to design activities that teach words and their uses to your child.

Language experience activities that are based on your child's experiences can help teach the words and the concepts they represent. For example, your child's SLP may plan language activities around a class trip to the bakery. All of the vocabulary, such as "oven," "bread," and "baker", would be taught; then the group would go to the bakery. The SLP could then point out all of the vocabulary taught in the class in their actual work setting. Your child would see what things like a bread oven, dough mixer, cookies, cake, and cash register are. After the trip, the SLP and your child could write (or dictate to you) a story about the trip. In subsequent therapy sessions, she might re-read the story or act out the trip to the bakery. This is an excellent way of making language learning concrete and real for your child.

Another method for teaching vocabulary is sometimes called the "unit plan." In this approach, the SLP works with your child's classroom teacher to combine language therapy with what your child learns in school. For example, if your child's class is studying weather or the seasons, the vocabulary taught in therapy would be directly related to the concepts taught in the unit, such as clouds, rain, winter, cold, and snow. This method for teaching vocabulary is especially useful in the older elementary school grades and as part of an inclusion model because the material used in therapy teaches and reinforces the material used in class. In the SLP sessions, the vocabulary taught is directly drawn from the reading, science, and other textbooks or workbooks your child may be using in classroom learning. For math, the SLP might work on explaining word problems, and translating them into simpler vocabulary. For children with Down syndrome in programs focusing on "life skills," the "unit" approach might focus on the language and speech used in food shopping, grooming, or housekeeping.

Pragmatics

Because pragmatics involve social interaction, these skills are best taught in small group therapy. Pragmatic therapy can cover the many different conversational skills your child will need. For example, she may need help learning the social situations in which informal and formal language should be used, how to ask for help, and how to start and end conversations. There are comprehensive published therapy programs for pragmatics such as *Functional Communicative Competence* and specifically targeted programs such as *Conversations*.

In teaching pragmatics, the SLP will probably use role playing, simulations, games, and activities. A specific technique that might be used is barrier games. In these games for two or more people, a physical barrier, such as a portable screen, is put between the communicating partners. One tries to send a message and the other tries to follow the message without any visual cues. For example, one child will make a sandwich or arrange a group of colored forms in a pattern just by following the verbal instructions given by the other child. When the activity is completed, the barrier is taken away, the results are checked, and the inaccuracies are discussed. Why did Kathy use whole wheat bread while you used white bread? Joey just said bread, and you didn't ask her "Which kind of bread?" Children generally enjoy these games, which provide very potent demonstrations of the need for clear directions and the need to ask for information.

One of the pioneers in teaching pragmatics in language therapy for children with Down syndrome is Dr. James MacDonald of Ohio State University. He advocates that SLPs use a conversation model for language intervention. MacDonald believes that all behavior communicates, including eye contact and gestures, and that movements communicate messages. He further believes that we should always interpret child behavior as communicative. MacDonald suggests that teaching must be at the level at which each child can succeed. SLPs should only expect that level of output from a child, but the models and expansions provided by you should be slightly more complex than your child's current skill level. MacDonald believes that the key to language success is a great deal of practice in social interactions in real situations. Thus, home practice must support the pragmatic skills being worked on in therapy.

Other Areas of Language Intervention

There are other language skills beyond morphology, syntax, semantics, or pragmatics that SLPs can work on with your child. These goals can include increasing your child's receptive language skills, enhancing her auditory memory, or improving her listening skills. Therapy might also seek to help your child learn to follow instructions of increasing length. This material might be taught through drills, word games, role playing and simulations, and reading and discussing a story. Language is a very complex task, and therapy may work on selected areas of language, with the goal of increasing overall communication competence. Therapy to improve expressive language skills might involve increasing the length of utterance or the number of turns in a conversation.

There are many other approaches to speech and language therapy that your child's SLP may suggest. For example, some authorities use reading and writing to teach language. There are many different theories about how children with Down syndrome learn best, and many different approaches to speech and language therapy. Knowledge is still growing, and more will be known about the best way to teach children with Down syndrome.

Be sure to ask the SLP working with your child for regular feedback on what your child is doing in therapy. Request a home activities program to reinforce the material being learned in therapy. If possible, observe your child's therapy sessions frequently, so that you can apply the language learned into your child's daily life.

Technology and Language Therapy

Technological advances have affected language therapy dramatically during last the decade in two major ways. First, communication using computers and other assistive and augmentative communication devices has made communication possible for people who cannot use speech; this use of technology is described in Chapter 8. Second, computers have been used in communication therapy to help teach concepts such as opposites and adverbs, and with a speech synthesizer to help teach verbal and written language skills. This section discusses the use of computers in language therapy, and also provides resources for using computers at home to help children with communication development. Some of the software is expensive and is therefore most often used in a professional setting.

Computers are not people. They cannot replace SLPs or teachers. They cannot prescribe therapy or establish goals. But, they do provide a very effective means for teaching and reinforcing concepts. Computers are exciting for children; they are part of almost every child's experiences today. Typically, developing children and children with Down syndrome can share their experiences with computers; they can talk about their newest game, and what they can do on the computer. Computers receive good press; children feel that computers are fun. Consequently, they are a powerful learning tool that can be used effectively as part of the language therapy program.

What are the benefits to using computers with children?

- Computers provide a visual display and visual reinforcement. Children with Down syndrome often learn best visually, so the computer capitalizes on these strengths.
- Computers provide for repetition and practice. Your child can repeat an item or a program as many times as she wants, providing the opportunity for as many practice sessions as she needs to learn a skill.
- Computers usually provide immediate reinforcement so that your child knows whether she has correctly answered the question. Computers may be programmed to repeat or re-teach an item if your child incorrectly answers the question.
- Computers generally maintain the interest of the user. They are engaging and fun for kids to use.
- Computer work can be highly individualized.
- In a world that increasingly involves computers, from voice mail to paying bills, children need to be comfortable with computers to be able to be independent as adults in the future.

- Computers allow the user to be an independent learner. Your child with Down syndrome can gain a sense of independence and build self-esteem.

A computer system that includes a speech synthesizer that converts computer commands into artificial speech, a touch window that allows your child to respond by pressing on the screen, and a power pad (an alternate keyboard) can provide most of the support needed for the most frequently used software.

Software is helpful for practicing specific concepts (First Verbs, Stickybear Opposites). For example, a bear that is "near" and a bear that is "far" away on the screen help teach or reinforce the specific concept. You can then reinforce this learning through other experiences, such as on the playground. Once your child is able to use the programs in therapy, she should be able to use the same programs at home because most are very user friendly. The SLP can advise you on which programs are most appropriate for the skills being targeted in therapy. A list of suggested software appears at the end of this chapter.

Legislation and Speech-Language Pathology Services

Since the passage of Public Law 94-142 in 1975, (also known as the Education for All Handicapped Children Act or EHA), each state has been required to provide services to meet the special educational needs of children with handicapping conditions. Under the law and regulations, these services must include speech and language therapy when needed. Along with other services, speech and language services are referred to as "related services." The EHA was amended in 1990 and is now called the Individuals with Disabilities Education Act (IDEA). The IDEA expanded the related services mandated by PL 94-142 to include assistive technology services such as augmentative communication.

For every child in school who is identified as needing special services, an Individualized Educational Program (IEP) must be developed for each special service provided. The IEP should include:

- speech and language therapy goals;
- intensity or type of service (individual, group, class);
- frequency of sessions per week; and
- length of each session.

Under the IDEA, services are provided at no cost by the school if your child meets the guidelines.

For children with Down syndrome birth to age three, another federal law establishes their right to services, including speech and language therapy, if they need them. These infants receive early intervention services. Instead of an IEP, an Individual Family Service Plan (IFSP) is used, and sometimes services are provided by an agency other than your local school district.

The IEP and IFSP are reviewed on an annual basis to determine eligibility for services, to evaluate progress, and to re-set goals. If speech and language services are denied, it does not mean that your child does not "need" speech and language services or could not benefit from them; it means that the school system, according to its guidelines, legally is not required to provide the services. These entrance and exit guidelines may not work best for children with Down syndrome, but they are widely used to determine eligibility for services.

Eligibility for Services

If your child is an infant or toddler, she will probably qualify for speech and language services simply because she has Down syndrome. If your child is three or older, however, a variety of criteria will be used to determine whether she is eligible for speech and language therapy. The developmental model for assessment and intervention is most commonly used for determining eligibility. This model looks at the age at which typical children develop speech and language skills. These ages, or "norms," are then used to evaluate your child's development. If your child's speech and language development is slower than the "norms," therapy is considered. This method puts parents of children with Down syndrome in a Catch-22 situation. If your child has been doing well in speech or language development for the past several months, she may score "at age level." That is, her speech and language skills may match her chronological age (C.A.) or mental age (M.A.) level. Based on her scores, speech and language services will be denied; she will be declared ineligible for services. The services may only be reinstated a year or two later, when she may be far enough below the developmental norm, and can qualify for services. Parents certainly want to hear that their child's speech and language are developing well, but if she is doing well, services will often be denied. Do not assume that your child does not need services just because the services are not being provided through the school system.

Another eligibility criterion sometimes used for children with developmental disabilities, including Down syndrome, is to require that their language scores be at a certain level below their cognitive scores in order to qualify for language services. If your child's language and cognitive scores are at approximately the same level, you are told that her language level is commensurate with her intelligence or overall cognitive level, and that services will not be provided. This creates another Catch-22 situation. Because most intelligence and cognitive testing is based on language ability (both to understand and follow the instructions and to answer questions), standardized test results may show that language and cognitive abilities are at the same level. The *real* question of whether your child needs language therapy is not answered. This criterion should not be used as a reason to declare your child with Down syndrome ineligible for speech and language services.

If you have concerns over your child's articulation or language development and feel that she "needs" services, seek an evaluation from an SLP outside of the school system. Many speech pathologists are in private practice. Comprehensive Down syndrome centers, health departments, private practitioners, and university training programs are all possible providers of speech and language services. Often, services provided through the health department or university training programs are subsidized and are provided at low cost to the family. Scholarships or sliding scale payment schedules may also be available. Some health insurance policies cover speech language pathology services, but others will only pay for an evaluation and will not cover ongoing services.

Where to Find Services

It is often difficult to locate the agency or program that can tell you whether your child qualifies for speech and language therapy under the IDEA. There is, however, one good place to start. Names and addresses for the agencies providing information about services under the IDEA in your state can be obtained from the National Information Center for Children and Youth with Disabilities (NICHCY) at 202-416-0300. Call to request a free copy of the *State Resource Sheet* for where you live.

If your child has been denied speech and language therapy under the IDEA, or if you would like her to receive private therapy in addition to the therapy provided by her school, there are several ways to locate qualified SLPs. The SLP in the local school, the chairperson of a local university training program, the administrator or developmental pediatrician at a comprehensive center, or your local parent support group may be able to recommend speech and language professionals in your area who have experience in working with children with Down syndrome.

Conclusion

Your child has a lot to gain from working with a skilled, committed SLP. As her parent, so do you. A SLP can guide you in working with your child in the ways that best nurture her speech and language development, and can make your daily communication with your child easier. If you and your child's SLP have frequent and open communication about problems and solutions, your child stands to get the most out of the services she receives. Speech and language therapy is not easy, and there are no instant "cures," but hard work and perseverance usually pay off. Learn as much as you can about how your child's SLP works with your child, and you will learn how better to work with your child yourself. And always remember that your child's SLP relies on you to tell her how to best work with your child. The insight and personal knowledge of your child that you contribute to the SLP is absolutely critical to the success of therapy. Work as a team.

Resources

National Information Center for Children and Youth with Disabilities
P.O. Box 1492
Washington, D.C. 20013-1492
202-884-8200
800-695-0285

American Speech-Language-Hearing Association
10801 Rockville Pike
Rockville, MD 20852-3279
1-800-638-8255
Consumer help line can provide information about specific speech and language problems. ASHA can also provide lists of speech and language resources in your state.

Suggested Readings

Buckley, S. and Sacks, B. (1987) *The Adolescent with Down Syndrome: Life for the Teenager and for the Family*. Portsmouth Down's Syndrome Trust. Portsmouth Polytechnic Institute, King Charles Street, Portsmouth, England UK PO1 2ER. Background information about language and reading.

MacDonald, J. (1985) "Language through Conversation: A Model for Intervention with Language-Delayed Persons." In Warren, S. and Rogers-Warren, A. *Teaching Functional Language*. Austin, TX:PRO-ED. This book provides information on the ECCO approach to conversational therapy.

Meyers, L. (1986) "Teaching Language," *Exceptional Parent*, November, 20-23.

Meyers, L. (1988) "Using Computers to Teach Children with Down Syndrome Spoken and Written Language Skills." In L. Nadel (ed.) *The Psychobiology of Down Syndrome*. Cambridge, MA: The MIT Press. Meyers's articles discuss the use of computers in speech, language, and writing.

O'Connor, L. & Schery, T. (1986) "A Comparison of Microcomputer-Aided and Traditional Language Therapy for Developing Communication Skills in Nonoral Toddlers. *Journal of Speech and Hearing Disorders*, *51*, 356-361.

Tanenhaus, J. (1991) *Home-Based Computer Program for Children with Down Syndrome* (3 volumes are available in the series: Facts and Information, Computer Software Guide, and Summary and Suggestions for Program Replication). Order from National Down Syndrome Society, 666 Broadway, Suite 810, New York, NY 10012, 1-800-221-4602. Inexpensive, helpful booklets.

Wilner, J. (1989) *Using Computers to Help Children with Down Syndrome*. New York: National Down Syndrome Society. (See above.)

Suggested Software

(All are available for the Apple II and IBM computers unless otherwise noted)
Laureate Learning Systems
110 E. Spring Street
Winooski, VT 05404
Excellent software for reinforcing language concepts. Graphics, pacing, and reinforcers are well done. Programs include:
First Categories
First Verbs
First Words
First Words II
Talking Nouns I
Talking Nouns II

Springboard Software
7808 Creekridge Circle
Minneapolis, MN 55435
Early Games for Young Children: alphabet and shape recognition; name
spelling; count, add, and subtract numbers 0-9; suggestions for extended
activities; picture menu.

MECC
3490 Lexington Ave, N.
St. Paul, MN 55126
First Letter Fun
Available for Apple II and IIGS; not available for IBM. Teaches association
of initial sounds of words to letters; 4 games; visual cuing and feedback
with animation; summary of correct responses; upper or lower case letters.

PEAL Software: *Programs for the Early Acquisition of Language*
P. O. BOX 8188
Calabasas, CA 91372
Exploratory Play and *Representational Play* are programs for early language stimulations, including teaching communicative intent. These
programs allow children to "ask for," "label," or "describe" a toy or action.
Keytalk is a program for children beginning to read and write. The user
types in letters, words, and sentences and the synthesizer "talks" the typed
information as it appears on the screen. Children can save and print their
stories.

Weekly Reader Family Software
c/o Scholastic
2931 E. McCarty St.
Jefferson City, MO 65102
In *Stickybear ABC,* the user selects a letter; songs and animated pictures
reinforce the sound association with user's selection. In *Stickybear Opposites,* the user controls animated characters' action of opposite concepts; auditory (music) and visual (animation) cuing and feedback
provided. In *Stickybear Shapes,* the user matches shapes and watches
animation; visual reinforcement through animation.

11 | COMMUNICATION NEEDS IN SCHOOL AND THE COMMUNITY

Communication does not occur only in therapy sessions or during assessments; your child communicates in his world. Two critical parts of that world are your child's school and community. The speech and language skills and problems discussed in earlier chapters all appear in school and the community. In addition, these two settings each have their own speech and language demands that challenge all children to learn and adapt. This chapter reviews the communication skills needed for success in school and in the community.

Many of the skills needed in the two settings, such as conversational skills, are similar, but there are also differences between the skills needed for academic success and those needed for interpersonal or social success. School places new demands on children with Down syndrome. The skills that have been mastered through the joint efforts of your child, you, and the speech-language pathologist (SLP) have built the foundation for successful communication in school, but as your child gets older, learns more, progresses in grade level, and moves from less integrated to more inclusive settings, the need for more advanced communication skills increases.

Language and Speech Needs in the Preschool Years

When a placement decision for preschool or kindergarten is being considered, parents usually ask whether their child's speech and language skills are adequate for the new situation. There are published lists of school survival skills (Wisconsin Day Care Survival Skills, Wisconsin Kindergarten Survival Skills, Hawaii Kindergarten Survival Skills) that shed light on which specific communication skills are important for early school performance. The skill which appears on each list and seems to be considered paramount by teachers for early school success is "Follows general rules and routines." Other communication skills that have been identified as important to school success in the early years are:

- Expresses wants and needs;
- Understands and complies with specific directions given by an adult;
- Takes turns;
- Interacts verbally with peers;
- Interacts verbally with adults;
- Focuses attention on speaker/ makes eye contact and listens; and
- Knows and recognizes his name.

In understanding skills like following rules it helps to examine what that skill includes. The ability to follow rules may involve communication skills such as understanding what is being asked, or the ability to do what is being asked, but it may also involve behavior. The ability to complete a worksheet may involve understanding the instructions and having the skills to complete the task, but may also involve the motivation and desire to complete the worksheet.

Being able to follow rules is important to school success, and the first step in learning to follow rules is understanding the concept of a "rule." How can you help? Most families have definite rules, and it is essential that the child understand that these are "rules." Discuss your rules frequently and be sure to label them as rules. For example, "We don't go in the street; that's the rule," or "We don't eat food in the living room; that's the rule." Whenever someone in the family breaks the rule, note that fact, by saying, for example, "Jacob, you shouldn't be eating a hot dog in the living room. We don't eat food in the living room. That's the rule." When your child is enrolled in a play group or preschool program, try to find out what the rules are, and reinforce those school rules at home. For example, "Brian, at school, you have to stand in line to go to the bathroom. That's the school rule. At home, you can go in if no one else is using the bathroom." If there are a limited number of rules, and your child has difficulty learning them, you can make a chart. Use photographs to illustrate the rules and briefly list the rules. Place a smiley face or a star on the chart each time your child remembers to follow the rule.

The communication skills cited by preschool teachers happen to be the very skills that are usually addressed in early language intervention programs, and are usually part of the follow-up activities SLPs suggest for parents to do at home. Many of the home activities suggested in earlier chapters focus on the communication skills important for school. Your child will probably have mastered many of these general skills. But, it is most important to determine whether the *specific* level of skill required in a *specific* school is a good match for the level of your child's communication abilities. For example, if your child's school focuses on reading and writing skills, even at the preschool and kindergarten level, does your child have the skills needed? If the school promotes the individual child working alone on tasks, would this be a good match for your child's skills and needs or would a social-interactive environment better meet your child's needs?

In exploring the best speech and language match for your child with Down syndrome, there are many things you can do. Talk with the early intervention specialists in your area. They probably have experience with the local preschool and elementary school programs in the area. They can provide direction and advice. The SLP who knows your child may be able to observe a particular program with you to determine whether the program would be a good match with your child's communication abilities. You want your child to have good models and language stimulation. Some programs may not allow interaction, but may instead focus on completing a motor, sorting, or pre-math task, and then going on to the next task without talking. Some programs have playtime and a social interaction time; other programs do not. Talk to parents who have had children in different programs in your area, and talk with them about how the individual programs met or failed to meet their childrens' needs. You can also talk with parents who have had children in a specific program recently, and inquire about the director and specific teachers. Observe in the school and, if possible, in the specific classroom. Talk with the director, and if possible, bring your child to visit the class, and observe the communication interaction between the teacher and your child. Then, consult with your early intervention team so that they can help you make an informed decision.

There are additional communication considerations in finding a good preschool for your child with Down syndrome. Sometimes parents wonder whether they should consider their child's speech intelligibility when choosing a preschool program. Will their child be at a disadvantage in a mainstreamed program if his speech is not easily understood outside his family? Usually, decisions about inclusion should *not* be based on whether your child's speech is understandable. The fact is, many *typically developing* preschoolers have intelligibility problems and dysfluencies between the ages of three and five. In addition, preschool activities are often structured so that much of the action focuses on the here and now. Because of this, teachers, parents, and other children can focus on the context of the communication and can frequently figure out what your child is trying to say and successfully decode his message. At this age, your child's communication partners are more patient and more willing to try to figure out what he is saying. If your child has the language needed for his school setting and can follow the rules and routines, he will generally do well even if it is difficult to understand his speech.

Language and Speech Needs in the Elementary School Years

Communication is at the core of learning in school. Communication occurs constantly from student to teacher, from teacher to student, and from student to student. In contrast to the communication skills needed for preschool success, the communication skill areas that are needed for successful communication in elementary school are more complex. They include:

- Understands and follows classroom routines;
- Is able to deviate from the routines when necessary;
- Participates in peer routines at lunch, recess, and in class;
- Has knowledge of topics (introducing, sustaining);
- Understands turn-taking rules, including:

  Takes turns appropriately in conversation,
  Knows how to request a turn,
  Uses appropriate greetings for different situations;

- Is able to follow teacher's instructions;
- Is able to decode and understand the teacher's cues;
- Is able to answer questions;

- Is able to share information;
- Understands the teacher's expectations for performance in an activity;
- Understands the teacher's expectations for the form and complexity of a response;
- Is able to repair conversational breakdowns:

    Requests for clarification ("What did you say?"),
    Requests for specification ("What did you mean?"),
    Requests for confirmation ("Is this what you said and   meant?");

- Has metalinguistic skills (can use terms to describe language such as how many sounds are in a word, what is the first sound, and how many syllables are in the word)
- Has metacomprehension skills (can understand language and learn material based on experience, reading, or class discussion);
- Understands idiomatic and abstract language ("take a chair," "it's raining cats and dogs").

In school, children with Down syndrome often need the assistance of a speech-language pathologist for general skills such as following directions and giving responses, requesting clarification and further information, and interacting on the playground. They may also need help with some specific skills, such as understanding and using the language of the curriculum. The teacher needs the professional expertise provided by the speech-language pathologist, for assistance in modifying the language of directions, or the curricular materials. For example, if your child has difficulty with math word problems, is it a difficulty with math or a problem with the language? If the teacher makes the language of the problem less complex, can your child solve the problem? On a multiple choice test, is your child having difficulty because he doesn't know the material or because he doesn't understand the concept, "all of the above" or "none of the above?" Your child may need to understand the concept of sound versus alphabet letter; for example, the /c/ in the word "city" and the /c/ in the word "cow" are two different sounds. The SLP can help him master the concept, so your child will be prepared to work on phonics in the classroom. Ways in which SLPs can provide assistance for your child and his teacher with the language demands of the curriculum are discussed later in this chapter.

As your child progresses through the elementary school years, the language demands of the curriculum increase. In kindergarten and first grade, children learn the basic skills of reading. Language development and language arts skills (reading, writing, comprehension, vocabulary) are one of the major focuses of the curriculum; so, when a word or concept is introduced, the teacher provides experiences to help the children learn about the word. Vocabulary is discussed and experienced, and the books used as readers have a limited vocabulary. By second and third grade, children are expected to have mastered the basic vocabulary word lists, such as the Dolch word list—the two hundred basic words most commonly used in readers, such as "a," "an," "about," "if," and "that." These are words children need to learn visually and cannot sound out; they are not, however, concept words. Children are also expected to have mastered vocabulary concepts of similarities and differences, comparative and superlative, and all and none, as well as the phonic skills needed for reading. In fourth and fifth grade, the focus moves from acquiring skills to using those skills. No longer are reading books based on a specific vocabulary; they are literature-based. Children are expected to master metalinguistic and metacomprehension skills. That is, they need to be able to use language for learning and to be able to talk about language on an abstract level. In fourth and fifth grade, the focus is on content and comprehension. Activities might address inference, prediction, or cause and effect, as well as higher level thinking skills. In addition, by the fourth grade children usually use separate textbooks for science and social studies, and these books are typically written at a much higher vocabulary and comprehension level than the fourth and fifth grade reading level. So, your child is being asked to use language to learn and master specific concepts; basic language and reading skills are expected to be mastered by this stage.

Many different types of learning situations occur in the classroom. Each presents its own communication demands. For example, a teacher-directed lesson on how to write a letter will have different communication requirements than an independent writing assignment. The ability to listen attentively and process instructions, however, is a skill that is needed in many different classroom situations. Children with Down syndrome may have difficulty following long and complex directions, especially those presented verbally, so you and the SLP can work with your child's classroom teacher to use shorter directions and to provide visual cues whenever possible. In addition, during the elementary school years, your child spends much of his day listening to the teacher talk. This differs greatly from life outside of school, where there is a more even distribution between listening and talking. Listening, remembering, and following verbal instructions are major parts of school. Auditory skills are stressed, and this may be difficult for children with Down syndrome who often learn better visually or with a multisensory approach.

In some classroom situations, instructions are clearly stated. Sometimes, your child can listen and clearly know what the expectations are for a task, but at other times, the requirements are not clearly stated. Teachers often make judgments and grade students on "hidden requirements." For example, is a one-word answer sufficient when asked to define "cat"? When the speech-language pathologist and the classroom teacher collaborate, they can search out the *stated* and *hidden* language requirements of each lesson, and help your child to know what is expected so that he can succeed. Children with Down syndrome may have the skills to answer a classroom question adequately and appropriately as long as they understand what they need to include in the answer.

The values of the school are generally the values of what is called a "low-context society." This means that the school values individualistic and independent performance, completion of tasks on schedule, long-term planning, order, and teacher control of verbal turn-taking (raising your hand, not calling out). In order to perform successfully in school, your child must know the "rules of the game." In the special education setting, the rules are usually clearly stated. As your child progresses to more inclusive settings, the rules for success are often hidden. The teacher does not purposely hide the requirements for success. The teacher, herself, often has not consciously recognized these hidden requirements. For example, what constitutes a "good" or a "poor" answer to a question? Here are two school-based question-and-answer scenarios:

1:

Teacher: What day is today?

Student: Friday.

2:

Teacher: What do we do on Friday?

Student: Go to school.

Class laughs.

Teacher: That's not a good answer.

In the first scenario, there is a good match between the answer the teacher is looking for and the answer the child gives. In the second scenario, the teacher wants a longer, more detailed answer such as, "We go to music, we change the calendar, we take a spelling test, we feed the hamsters, we clear our desks for the weekend." But, the teacher did not give any clues—she did not say, "Can someone tell me *all* of the things that we do on Friday? or "Can you tell me *three* things that we do every Friday?" Your child with Down syndrome may have been able to tell three events or even five events that are part of the schedule on Friday, if he knew what he was supposed to include in his answer. When the classroom teacher and the speech-language pathologist work together, they can help each other make the classroom requirements more understandable for your child and increase his opportunities to successfully match the teacher's expectations.

During the elementary school years, speech intelligibility often presents a problem for children with Down syndrome. Yet intelligible speech is essential to academic success and to inclusion. Intelligibility of speech should be considered when making decisions on inclusion and school placement. Consult your speech-language pathologist for an evaluation of the factors affecting your child's speech intelligibility, and request services to address the intelligibility problem. Chapter 8 discusses speech intelligibility in detail.

How can you, your child's SLP, and classroom teachers work together to help your child achieve his potential during the school years? Four new trends in speech-language pathology have emerged to meet the needs of children and teachers who are trying to make inclusive education work:

- classroom-based therapy;
- curriculum-based therapy;
- collaborative consultation;
- whole language model.

Although these methods of providing services may be used for speech treatment as well, they are more widely used in language therapy. In the past, therapy was almost always done outside of the classroom, in separate sessions. This method for service delivery is now referred to as "pull-out therapy." Today there is a trend toward providing speech and language therapy in the classroom. With classroom-based therapy, the therapy might involve the entire class or may be conducted with a small group within the classroom. Each method of providing services has its strengths and weaknesses. For children with Down syndrome, individual pull-out therapy is better for working on muscle exercises and oral skills, articulation, and intelligibility, while classroom-based therapy works well for semantic and pragmatic skills. Another recent trend is to coordinate therapy with your child's academic curriculum. That is, vocabulary taught in therapy would be based on the material in the educational curriculum. For example, if your child is learning about the human body in science, the SLP might help him learn such words as "skeleton," "muscles," and "respiration." A third trend is for the classroom teacher and the SLP to collaborate to help the child succeed. This is referred to as the collaborative consultation model. In this method the SLP helps the classroom teacher learn how best to give instructions to children with Down syndrome or how best to phrase problems. Yet another trend is called the "whole language model." Speaking, listening, reading, and writing are viewed as integrated skills which comprise the overall communication skill that your child needs to learn, rather than as separate and discrete skills. The classroom teacher, reading specialist, and SLP all work together to plan curriculum units that use all communication skill areas to help your child learn. For example, your child's class may be learning about bears. The class would read books about bears, talk about bears, go to the zoo, see a video about bears, sing a song about bears, write a story about bears, and make teddy bear cookies.

You can work with the SLP and the classroom teacher to practice the skills, and to learn the language concepts demanded by the curriculum. Try to be proactive; that is plan ahead for what your child will need to learn. If you know that your child's class will be talking about the explorers, plan family trips to historical locations, take out videos and library books, have an explorer's party or explorers's day, make a board game about the explorers. If your child's class is learning about rooms in a house, furniture, and household objects, take a field trip to a furniture store, play with dollhouses and toy furniture, or look through magazines and cut out picture of objects that would go in each room in your house. Then, put them in a photo album as a "book" about your house. There is an almost unlimited variety of "whole language" activities. Your child may need additional experience to learn, but your child can be a successful student.

Communication Skills in the Community

Communication is interacting with people in real life. Life in the community is life with your family, your neighbors, your friends, the kids in Cub Scouts and Brownies, the children and adults in your church or synagogue, the people in the supermarket. This is your child's world, made up of the people who surround him. The speech skills that your child needs in his community are similar in some ways to those he needs for school. As in school, people in the community need to be able to understand your child to interact directly with him. In many situations, in both school and in the community, understandable speech is extremely important. Speech and language also need to be appropriate. For example, it would be inappropriate to shout in church, or to use very formal speech in Cub Scouts or Brownies with your friends. But, there the similarity ends.

The language and communication demands of the community are very different from those of school. There is a lot more leeway in the community. There are actually many acceptable varieties of speech and language for interaction in the community. For example, if you ask a child with Down syndrome if he would like to go for pizza, he can flash a smile and give you the high five sign and you will know that the answer is yes, just as if he had said the word. In the neighborhood, appropriate responses may be gestural, such as shaking the head or shrugging the shoulders, or may be single words or sentences. The bottom line is that communication must be appropriate and communication interactions must follow the rules of pragmatics, the rules governing the social use of language in real life.

Language needs in real life are based on experiences, including shared experiences with parents, siblings, grandparents, cousins, and friends. We know that vocabulary can continue to grow throughout life and vocabulary acquisition is driven by your child's interests. If your child is going on a family trip to Disney World, the names of the Disney characters will be a natural part of the experience. If you are taking an airplane, the vocabulary of the airport, luggage, terminal, gate, and airplane will be a part of the experience. If your child likes to swim, the vocabulary of the sport will be of interest to your child. Baking, cooking, and crafts projects all have their own vocabularies. You can consult the vocabulary list in the appendix to Chapter 5 for suggested terms within specific categories.

Children learn vocabulary if it is of interest to them. Research tells us that children with Down syndrome continue to add words to their vocabularies well into adulthood and that children with Down syndrome have larger vocabularies than children with other developmental disabilities, matched for mental age level. For example, a child with Down syndrome with a mental age of seven usually has a bigger vocabulary than a child with autism or pervasive developmental disability with a mental age of seven. Vocabulary, then, can continue to increase if it is fueled by interests and experiences. Experiences in the community with family and friends provide an excellent basis for learning many new vocabulary words.

There are different types of communication situations in which communication skills are applied in the community. Some situations are unusual or unique, such as emergencies, but in daily life, much communication is repetitive and routine, such as greetings, good-byes, and questions directed toward children. These can be practiced as "routines" so that your child will be familiar with these situations. If your child learns the "script" for greeting people, he can use that script over and over again. In general, no one cares if you use the same greeting again and again; in fact, most people have standard meeting and departing greetings. Greetings are social rituals and aren't expected to be different or unique each time. "Hi," "hello," and "How're you doing" are all fine greetings. "See you later," "great to see you," and "bye-bye" are all fine departures. They don't need to vary, and your child will have the chance to practice them again and again so that these social routines will feel very comfortable. In general, people greet children, ask how they are, how old they are, where they go to school, what grade they are in, and perhaps what subjects they like best. These questions are meant to be answered briefly and routinely. When someone asks "How are you," they are not asking for a medical report, they are merely greeting you and touching base. So, if your child answers these general questions well, he will certainly hold up his end of the social greeting ritual.

Conversational skills are more complex and thus are more challenging for children with Down syndrome. These are the skills that children need and use regularly in daily life. Pragmatics and conversational skills are discussed in detail in Chapter 7. The goal is effective communication, and in the community, all communication systems (such as speech, gestures, facial expressions) can contribute to having your message understood.

Conclusion

Communication can either be your child's door to opportunity and experiences or it can be a barrier. Understanding the different demands that your child's school and community place upon his communication skills can help you focus your work with your child, his SLP, and his teacher. The last ten years have seen dramatic change in the participation of children with Down syndrome in school and in the community. There are now real opportunities for children to learn and play in the real world. Later, there are opportunities for working in their community. And what has fueled this change has been the ever-increasing abilities of people with Down syndrome, including their communication abilities. As more is learned about how to tap their potential (and just what the full extent of that potential is), people with Down syndrome will become even more integrated into their schools and communities. How you and your child's teachers and SLP work with your child will go far to opening the doors to inclusion throughout life for your child.

INDEX

Abstract thinking, 17, 48, 62

Adenoids, enlarged, 15, 152, 153

Allergies, 15, 151

American Speech-Language-Hearing Association, 4, 214

Apraxia, verbal, 141–42

Articulation, 15, 130, 136–46, 179–81, 197–201. *See also* Intelligibility

ASHA, 4

Assessments. *See* Evaluations

Attention span, 14, 90, 185

Auditory discrimination, 199

Auditory figure-ground skills, 123–24

Auditory memory, 16, 120–23

Auditory perception, 123

Auditory processing, 16, 120

Auditory skills, teaching, 119–24

Auditory stimulation 25–26, 39–40

Augmentative communication, 155–62. *See also* Total Communication

Baby talk, 29

Backing, 147

Barrier games, 206

Biklen, Douglas, 160

Boehm Test, 186

Books, suggested, 92–95. *See also* Reading

Breathing, 178

Bubbles, soap, 143

Carrier phrases, 85–86

Categories, 100

Cause and effect, 50–51

CCC, 194

CELF, 186

Center for Special Education Technology, 163

Certificate of Clinical Competence (CCC), 194

Child Find, 170

Chronological age, 180, 212

Clarifications, requesting, 118–19, 222

Clonic blocks, 135

Coarticulation, 201

Cognitive skills, 48–52. *See also* Mental retardation

Colds, 15

Communication. *See also* Language; Speech

abilities needed in community, 227–31

abilities needed in school, 217–27

appropriateness of, 228–29

definition of, 7

difficulties with, in children with DS, 9–20

foundation skills for, 24–29, 36–53

importance of, 1
preventing problems in, 196
remediating problems in, 196
Communication boards, 156–58, 165–66
Communicative intent, 50, 56, 106
Computers
as communication systems, 158–59
use of in therapy, 208–10, 215–16
Concepts. *See also* Semantics
list of, 71–77
teaching, 61–67
Conductive hearing loss, 10–11. *See also* Hearing problems
Conversational skills, 109–10, 124–27, 230. *See also* Pragmatics
Conversations, 206
Coordination, muscular, 202. *See also* Verbal apraxia
Crocker, Allen, 193
Crossley, Rosemary, 160
Cup drinking, 31
Cues, 67, 91, 224
Delays in responding, 18, 28
Deletions of sounds, 147
Diadochokinesis testing, 182–83
Digressing. *See* Topicalization
Directions, following, 125–26, 207, 221, 224
Distinctive feature analysis, 180–81, 199–200

Dolch word list, 223
Down syndrome
cognitive characteristics associated with, 16–17
effects of on communication skills, 1–2, 8, 9–20, 97–128, 130–53
hearing problems associated with, 10–11
physical characteristics associated with, 15
visual problems associated with, 11–12
Dysarthria, 140–41. *See also* Hypotonia
Dysfluency. *See* Fluency
Ear infections, 10–11, 26, 133
Early intervention programs, 23
Education for All Handicapped Children Act. *See* IDEA
EHA. *See* IDEA
Eligibility for speech therapy, 170, 180, 190, 211–13. *See also* IDEA
ENT, 133, 151
Evaluations, 169–91
case history component of, 173–74
formal vs. informal, 175–76
language skills assessed in, 184–88
observation component of, 174–75
parent's role during, 171–72
reasons for, 169–70

seeking private, 212–13
speech skills assessed in, 177–84
understanding results of, 188–89
Expressive language. *See* Language, expressive
Expressive One-Word Picture Vocabulary Test, 186
Eye contact, 36–37, 107
Facial expressions, 107–9
Facial structure, 177. *See also* Tongue
Facilitated communication, 160–62
Feeding, 29–32
Fluency, 15, 135–36, 178–79, 202. *See also* Intelligibility
Focusing eyes, difficulties in, 24
Fokes Sentence Builder, 204
Fronting, 147
Functional Communicative Competence, 206
Gaze
 reciprocal, 36–37, 107
 referential, 38–39
Generalization, 16, 65
"Gentle onset" method, 202
Gestures, 47–48, 229. *See also* Total Communication
Grammar. *See* Syntax
Greetings, 20, 47, 230. *See also* Pragmatics
Hawaii Kindergarten Survival Skills, 218

Hearing problems in children with DS, 10–11, 26, 133, 139. *See also* Auditory skills
Hugging, inappropriate, 104–6
Huskiness. *See* Voice quality
Hypernasality, 152, 201
Hyponasality, 151, 201
Hypotonia, 15, 30, 36, 133, 139–40. *See also* Dysarthria
IDEA, 210–13
Idioms, 124–25, 222
IEP, 211
IFSP, 211
Imitation. *See also* Cues
 of movements, 41–43
 of sounds, 28, 44–46
 testing abilities in, 181
 with expansion, 80–82
Inclusion, 226
Individualized Education Plan, 211
Individualized Family Service Plan, 211
Individuals with Disabilities Education Act. *See* IDEA
Infants, communication activities for, 24–29
Instructions, following. *See* Directions, following
Integration. *See* Inclusion
Intelligibility
 definition of, 15
 effects of DS on, 15, 130–53
 evaluating, 183

factors affecting, 131
increasing, 153–55
importance of, 129
needs for, in elementary
    school, 226
needs for, in preschool, 220
Intent. *See* Communicative intent
Interrupting, 110
Kinesics, 103–4. *See also* Gestures
Language. *See also* Communication
abilities needed in school,
    217–19, 223–26
assessment of, 184–88
components of, 98
definition of, 7
difficulties with, in children
    with DS, 97–128
expressive, 8, 186–87, 207
motivating child to learn,
    127–28
receptive, 8, 185–86, 207
receptive-expressive gap, 17–
    18, 187
therapy for problems with,
    203–10
Language boards, 156–58, 165–
    66
Learning style, 32–33
Linguistic precursors, 35–53
Lips, 181. *See also* Dysarthria;
    Facial structure

Listening. *See also* Auditory
    skills
activities for 25–26
to encourage child's speech,
    66
Localization to sound, 39–40
Loudness of speech, 133–35
Low context society, 224–25
Low muscle tone, 15, 30, 36,
    133, 139–40. *See also*
    Dysarthria
MacDonald, James, 207
Mainstreaming. *See* Inclusion
Mean length of utterance
    (MLU), 18, 186–87
Means-end, 51
Memory, auditory, 16, 120–23
Mental age, 180, 212
Mental retardation, 16–17. *See
    also* Cognitive skills
Metacomprehension skills, 222
Metalinguistic skills, 222
Mirrors, 24, 146
Mispronunciations. *See* Intelligibility; Phonological
    processes
MLU, 18
Modeling. *See* Imitation
Morphology, 100–2, 204
"Motherese," 29
Motivating child to learn, 127–
    28
Mouth
breathing through, 15, 151

size of, in children with DS, 15

Multisyllabic words. *See* Diadochokinesis testing; Dysarthria; Verbal Apraxia

Muscle coordination, 202. *See also* Verbal apraxia

Muscle tone, low. *See* Hypotonia

Muscles, strengthening exercises for, 201. *See also* Hypotonia; Tongue

Musical instruments, 144

Nasal voice quality, 152

National Down Syndrome Congress, 4

National Down Syndrome Society, 4

National Easter Seal Society, 163

National Information Center for Children and Youth with Disabilities, 5, 213, 214

NICHCY, 5, 213, 214

Noises, filtering out unimportant, 120, 123–24

Norms for sound production, 179–80, 189, 211

Nursing, 30

Object permanence, 48–50

Occupational therapists, 13, 28, 32

Omissions of sounds. *See* Articulation; Phonological processes

Oral peripheral examination, 177

Oro-motor therapy, 32

Otitis media. *See* Ear infections

Otolaryngologist, 133, 151

Pacing boards, 82–83, 131–33, 202

Palate. *See* Facial structure

Parents
and partnership with SLPs, 193, 194–95, 208, 213–14
as teachers, 2–3, 60–61
role of during evaluations, 171–72, 174–75

Peabody Picture Vocabulary Tests, 186

Phonemes, 136

Phonetic placement, 199

Phonic skills, 223

Phonological processes, 146–49, 183, 200–1

Phonology, 102

Phrases. *See also* Mean length of utterance
carrier, 85–86
prepositional, 86–87
three-word, 82–87
two-word, 79–82

Play and language learning, 87–89, 185

Pragmatics
activities for teaching, 103–19
and children with DS, 20
assessment of, 187–88

effects of, on intelligibility, 153
therapy for, 206–7
turn-taking, 46–47
types of, 103
Prefixes. *See* Morphology
Pre-language skills, 35–53
Prepositional phrases, 86–87
Preschool. *See* School
Presuppositions, 112
Prompts. *See* Cues
Pronunciation difficulties. *See* Intelligibility; Phonological processes
Proxemics, 104–6
Public Law 94–142. *See* IDEA
Rambling speech. *See* Topicalization
Rate of speech, 131–33, 202–3
Rattles, 26
Reading, 89–91, 223, 227. *See also* Books
Real-life activities, 62, 99, 128, 205
Receptive language. *See* Language, receptive
Receptive One-Word Picture Vocabulary Test, 186
Reciprocal gaze, 36–37
Referential gaze, 38–39
Reflexes, 140
Requests, 116–18
RESNA, 164

Resonance, 15, 151–52, 178, 201–2. *See also* Intelligibility
Respiration, 178
Reversals, of sounds, 141
Routines, following, 221
Rules, following, 218–19
School
choosing an appropriate, 219–20
communication skills needed for, 218–27
Scores, on speech/language tests, 189–90
Screeching, 25, 28
Semantics, 19, 98–100, 205–6
Sensorineural hearing loss, 11. *See also* Hearing problems
Sensory integration, 13–14
Sensory integration therapy, 13
Sensory skills, 9–14
Sentences. *See* Phrases
Sequenced Inventory of Communication Development, 184
Sequencing, 15. *See also* Intelligibility
Shouting, 133–35, 201
Sign languages, 58. *See also* Augmentative communication; Total Communication
Simplifications of sounds. *See* Articulation; Phonological processes
Singing, 43, 84–85

Slowed response, 18, 28
SLPs. *See* Speech-language pathologists
Software. *See* Computers
Songs. *See* Singing
Sounds
   attending to, 40
   filtering out unimportant, 120, 123–24
   locating source of, 39–40
   simplifications or substitutions of, 146–49
   stimulation of, 25–26, 39–40
Speech. *See also* Communication; Intelligibility
   age of development, in children with DS, 55
   assessment of, 177–83
   definition of, 8
   difficulties with, in children with DS, 8, 56, 130–53
   fluency of, 15, 135–36, 178–79, 202
   rapid, 131–33, 202–3
   therapy for problems with, 196–203
   volume of, 133–35
Speech and hearing associations, 5
Speech and language therapy, 193–216
   computer usage in, 208–10, 215–16
   eligibility for, 170, 180, 190, 211

   for articulation problems, 197–98
   for fluency problems, 202
   for morphology problems, 204
   for pragmatics problems, 206–7
   for rate problems, 202–3
   for semantics problems, 205–6
   for syntax problems, 204–5
   for voice and resonance problems, 201–2
   importance of, 193
   laws concerning, 210–13
   reasons for, 196, 203, 222–23
   seeking private, 213
   settings for, 194, 226–27
   types of, 197–203
Speech-language pathologists
   and partnership with parents, 193, 194–95, 208, 213–14
   assessment techniques of, 177–87
   qualifications of, 194
   role of, 3, 31, 59, 222–23, 224–27
Stimulability testing, 181–82
Stuttering. *See* Fluency
Stylistic variations, 110–11
Substitutions of sounds. *See* Articulation; Phonological processes
Suffixes. *See* Morphology

Surgery
  effects of on resonance, 152–53
  on tongue, 150
Syntax, 19, 102, 204
Syntax One, 204
Tactile problems in children with DS, 12–13, 32
Tactile stimulation, 26–27
Talking. *See* Speech
TASH, 164
Teachers, 222, 224–27
Technology. *See* Computers
Technology Assistance Projects, 164
Technology for Language and Learning, 164
Test of Language Development, 184
Tests, standardized, 175–76, 184, 186, 189–90
Token Test for Children, 186
Tongue
  control of, 177
  muscle tone of, 30, 140
  protruding or thrusting, 149–51
  size of, 15
Tonic blocks, 135
Topicalization, 113–16
Topics, switching. *See* Topicalization
Total Communication, 57–60, 81, 203. *See also* Augmentative communication

Touch
  difficulties with, 12–13
  inappropriate, 104–6
Tracking, 11, 37–38
Tube feeding, 32
Turn-taking, 28–29, 46–47, 112–13
Unit plan, 205
U.S. Society for Augmentative and Alternative Communication, 164
Velopharyngeal closure, 152, 178
Verb tenses. *See* Morphology; Syntax
Verbal apraxia, 141–42
Visual problems in children with DS, 11–12, 36
Visual stimulation, 24–25, 36–39
Vocabulary. *See also* Semantics
  list of important words, 71–77
  potential of children with DS to learn, 19, 99, 229
  teaching, 61–67, 98–99, 205, 229
  words used in school, 223
Voice quality, 151–52, 178, 201–2
Volume of speech, 133–35
Waisman Center, 164
Whistles, 143–44
Whole language model, 227

Wisconsin Day Care Survival
     Skills, 218
Wisconsin Kindergarten Sur-
     vival Skills, 218
Word endings. *See* Morphology;
     Phonological processes
Word retrieval problems, 16
Words, multisyllabic. *See*
     Diadochokinesis testing;
     Dysarthria; Verbal Apraxia

About the Author:

Libby Kumin, Ph.D., CCC-SLP, received her masters and doctorate in speech-language pathology from New York University. Since 1983, she has been the Chairperson of the Department of Speech-Language Pathology/Audiology at Loyola College in Baltimore, Maryland, where she founded the Speech and Language Intervention Program for Children with Down Syndrome. Among her numerous professional affiliations and honors, she is a member of the Professional Advisory Board for the National Down Syndrome Congress and an Associate Editor for *Down Syndrome Papers and Abstracts for Professionals.*